THE EMERGING

A Journey Of Love And Healing With Watercolor Flower Mandalas

50 MANDALAS & 50 POEMS

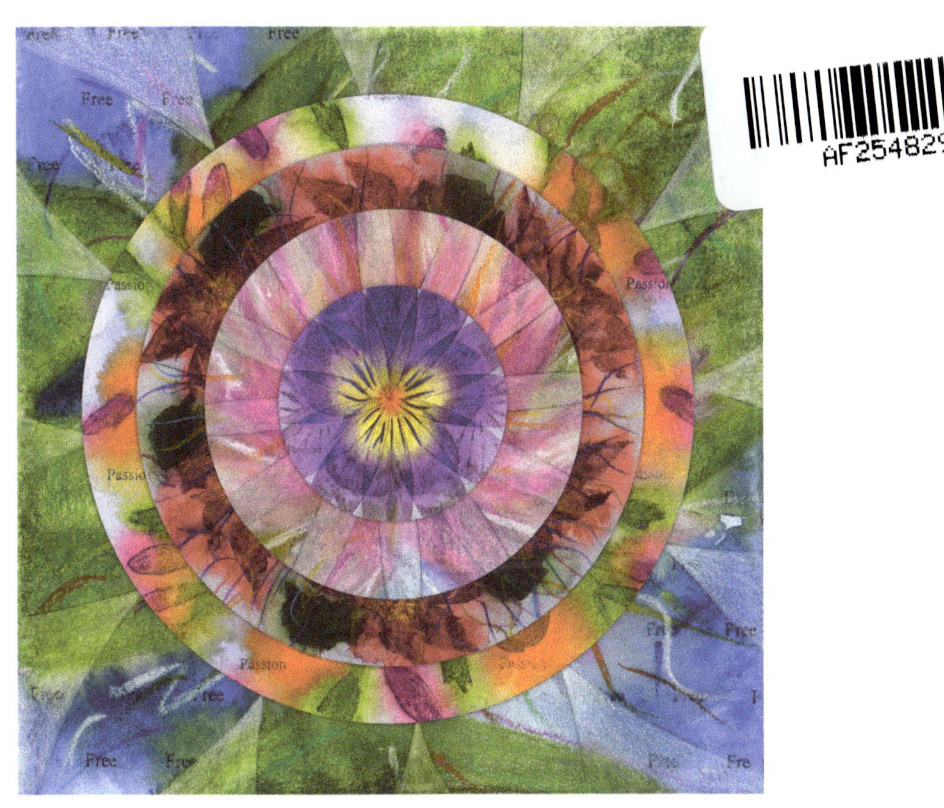

MICHELE FAIA
WWW.MICHELEFAIA.COM

AF254829

I WELCOME EVERY OPPORTUNITY
TO SPREAD LOVE, BLESSINGS AND ENCOURAGEMENT
OF HEART AND SPIRIT, FAR AND WIDE.
-Michele Faia

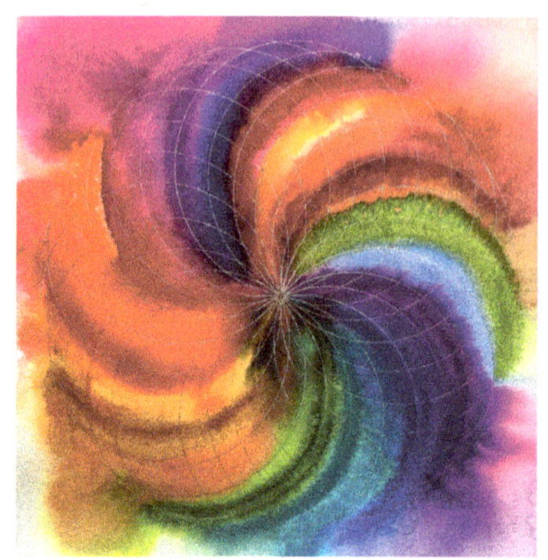

DEDICATED TO ALL WHO ARE EMERGING IN THE LIGHT

THE EMERGING; A Journey Of Love And Healing With Watercolor Flower Mandalas
Published by Michele Faia, Aptos, California

Copyright ©2022 by Michele Faia

All rights reserved. no part of this publication may be reproduced or utilized in any form or by any means without the prior written permission of the author.

The Emerging describes the personal experiences of the author and reflects her views. It is not intended as a guide to personal diagnosis or independent self-healing. no medical claim is made as to the effect of the exercises described in this book.

Creative Direction and Design: Don Faia

Formatting and Production: Anita Bonno Bernard

ISBN 978-0-578-35500-9

Table of Contents
FORWARD
INTRODUCTION
50 MANDALAS & 50 POEMS

GOODNESS

9

COMING OUT

11

BUDDING POTENTIAL

13

BEING OK AND NOT WRONG

15

INTERNAL HELP

17

GOD AS HYDRANGEA

19

TWIG VISION

21

MY SACRED SELF CHILD WITHIN

23

FLIGHT OF THE SOUL

25

NOURISHING BERRIES AND
NURTURING ANEMONES

27

CAMELLIA IS CARING

29

DYING TO BE BORN ANEW

31

SNOWBALL, INSPIRE THE BLUEBIRD TO
SING MY SWEETNESS INTO BEING

33

BURNING AWAY DEFEAT

35

GO FOR IT

37

STEP OUT OF THE DARKNESS AND INTO
THE LIMELIGHT

39

FIRST CHAKRA CIRCLE OF LOVE

41

NURTURING TURTLE

43

GRATITUDE

45

BLOOM! YOU ARE FREE

47

TRANSFORMATION: IN THE LAND OF THE FREE &
HOME OF THE BRAVE

49

HEALING WITH ROSES; LOOKING TO
SEE WHO I REALLY AM

51

THE HEALING FROM THE BROMELIAD

53

CYCLAMENS COMING OUT OF A BIG HEART

55

BUDDING

57

PASSION

59

THE HEALING OF THE DARKNESS FLOWER

61

FEEL IT TO HEAL IT

63

SHOW HER WHAT HELPS

65

THERE IS A HEALING GOING ON

67

THOUGHTS ARE THINGS

69

NURTURE ME WHERE I LIVE AND
LET ME FLY

71

RELEASE

73

THE FLOWERING OF ENCOURAGEMENT

75

AMARYLLIS, ANEMONE, LETTUCE
AND THE NEED FOR STARS

77

REACHING FOR THE LIGHT

79

THE OFFERING: OLIVE BRANCHES,
LIMELIGHT AND THE STAR

81

EXPANDING MY KALEIDOSCOPE VISION

83

BEAUTIFUL, SWEET AND MYSTERIOUS

85

MY EGG OF LIFE

87

FREE

89

PEACE

91

LOVE IN THE SEED OF LIFE

93

CONVOVULUS IS LOVE

95

YOU ARE LOVED FOR YOUR SPIRIT

97

BUTTERFLIES COMFORT ME ON MY
SACRED JOURNEY

99

HAPPY BIRTH DAY! GIVE ME FIVE!

101

I AM FREE, YOU ARE FREE

103

SHE MAKES MY HEART SING

105

SO MUCH LOVE

107

ABOUT THE PAINTINGS
108
ACKNOWLEDGEMENTS
119

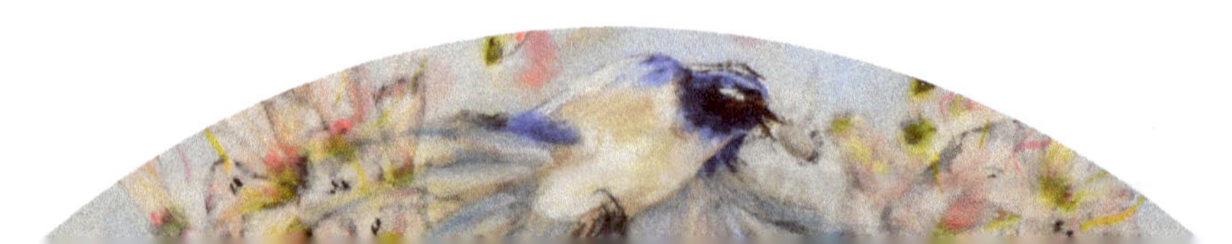

FORWARD

Marda Reid, M.A.

How would you like to find the divine essence of who you are? There is a path and Michele Faia can lead the way! *The Emerging* is a book that spans almost twenty years of deeply creative and spirit-filled paintings accompanied by poetry that both inspires and informs each of us to heal, love and emerge in the world as one's true self.

I met Michele Faia through her teaching of mandala painting. After several years in her classes, I became her teaching assistant. She became my mentor and my friend. I have always been awestruck by her painting and writing. Her brave heart is wide open and she showed me how to open mine. By painting mandalas, I learned about life, light and love. To this day, I pull out my paints to obtain insight and well-being. Her teaching has changed many lives, one mandala at a time.

Michele is the exemplar in exercising the concept of co-creation. For each painting, she writes on the back her intention to allow Spirit to participate in the interaction of paint and water on the page.

And the way this happens is something to behold! It is an act of alchemy where Michele and Spirit are in union. When you see the pages that follow, you will find flow, freedom, and radiance. She creates to obtain a greater understanding of a full range of emotions and to transform pain in its varied forms to a state of reawakening. This is a brave act and requires vision – seeing beyond her pain to the beauty that is always there.

This book can be read cover-to-cover or each page can be used individually as a daily affirmation. I would also suggest reading as if the "you" in each poem is "YOU," for there is a universal quality to the themes of Michele's writing. Above all, please read this book with your eyes wide open (third eye included!), your heart wide open, and without fear. Trust the direction of the images and the words. *The Emerging* is an invitation to YOU and to all of us to heal and we can.

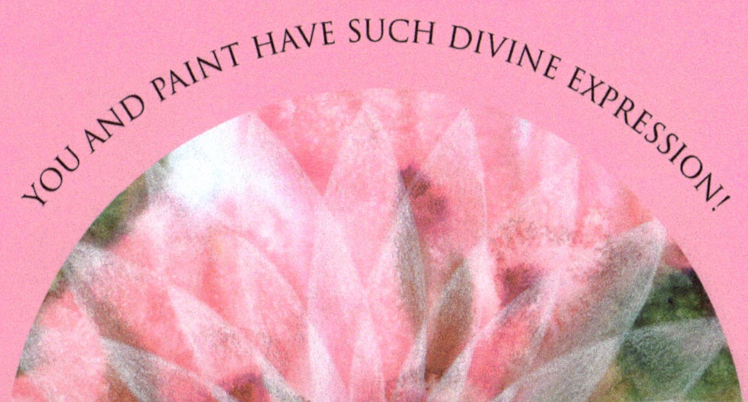

INTRODUCTION

Michele Faia

I discovered mandalas thirty years ago and what a find! I now paint them, teach watercolor mandala making and have written two previous books about their power and heart opening ability. I have also used them myself for healing.

What are they? The word mandala means circle or center, and very over simplified, they are a sacred circle representing a sacred journey. It's the biggest journey of all – to your heart, to your center, to your Spirit.

For me, mandalas have always involved flowers. Mandalas come to me as visions, flower mandala visions. Like flowers, mandalas are generally circular and symmetrical and always have a center. This book is fifty of my watercolor mandalas with poems as their back stories. These fifty are inspired by my love of flowers and watercolor and my communication with the flowers. I see flowers as a gift of beauty emerging to love us. Similarly, mandalas are also a gift, emerging to offer their unfathomable spiritual potential.

I started this book many years ago and originally called it "Healing Mandalas: How I Transformed from a Slug to a Butterfly." Clearly, I wasn't ready to write it so the book was shelved. Now tapped on the shoulder by Spirit and Divinely guided, I share my journey of traveling through a dark time and emerging in the light. I tell the story with "Flower Energy Paintings," the name my Spirit Guide once called my flower mandalas.

The story begins twenty years ago following my treatment for cancer which cracked me wide open and exposed all sorts of stuffed feelings and emotions. I was very depressed, was not painting or teaching and thought I'd lost those abilities. I sought help from a therapist. She told me that cancer had actually saved my life because if I had kept stuffing my feelings it would have killed me. She helped me sort out a very challenging past and we all came through it together – my Self, with the flowers and the mandalas. My therapist suggested I write a book telling how I survived the darkness, emerged in the light, and how it could be helpful for others. This is that book.

The writing of the book was so much fun, an inspired and wonderful experience. Each day I would visit what became my "magic bench" which overlooked the Pacific Ocean. I would receive a vision of a completed mandala and would return home to write a poem about the painting, with a new perspective, love and understanding of it and of my past.
I see the poems as an explanation of the bigger picture. The fifty mandalas are a record of my transformation and healing.

I present this book as an encouragement for the reader to do the same. I offer it as a torch of light for your emerging. Someone held the light for me and we are all together on this journey. We are ONE. Remember the flowers, which are an essential gift to us. Flowers have been my beautiful and willing teachers, and they can be for anyone – they are essential. They are our "saviors."

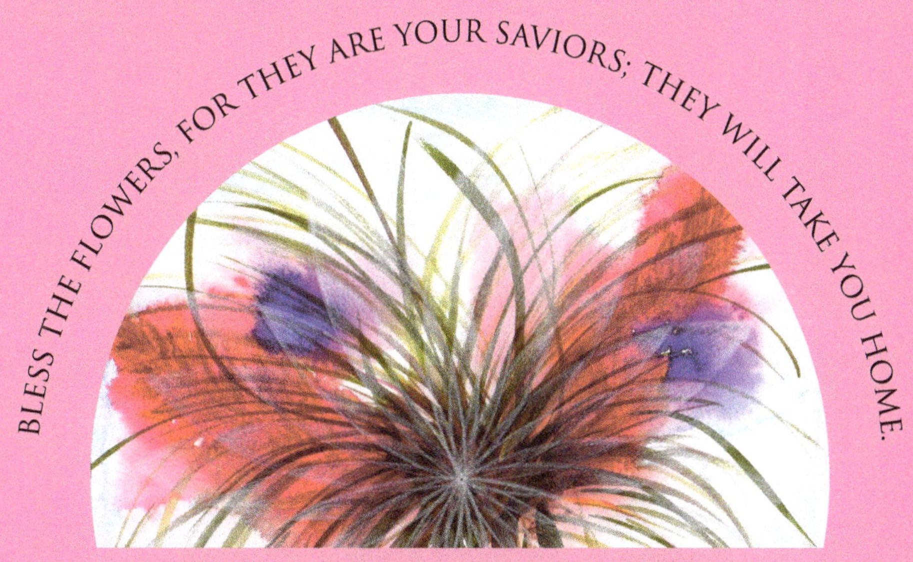

—Chief Seattle (from my dream)

GOODNESS

The sunflower is such a wonderful symbol.
I had a vision of my grandpa
taking me out to the fields,
to the fruit, to the walnuts,
the growing crops, the blue sky.
He talked to me and said,
"You can do this, you can heal.
You are special.
You are strong.
You are good.
You never have to experience
that pain again.
You will heal,
You can be yourself."
In the vision
a higher being stood at my side.
You are dearly, dearly loved.
Everything will work out,
You will heal.
We want your light!
That made me smile
and want to be my creative self.
The sunflower was part of my vision
and said it all about that little girl.
Her goodness, her light, her creativity
and the riches she has to offer.

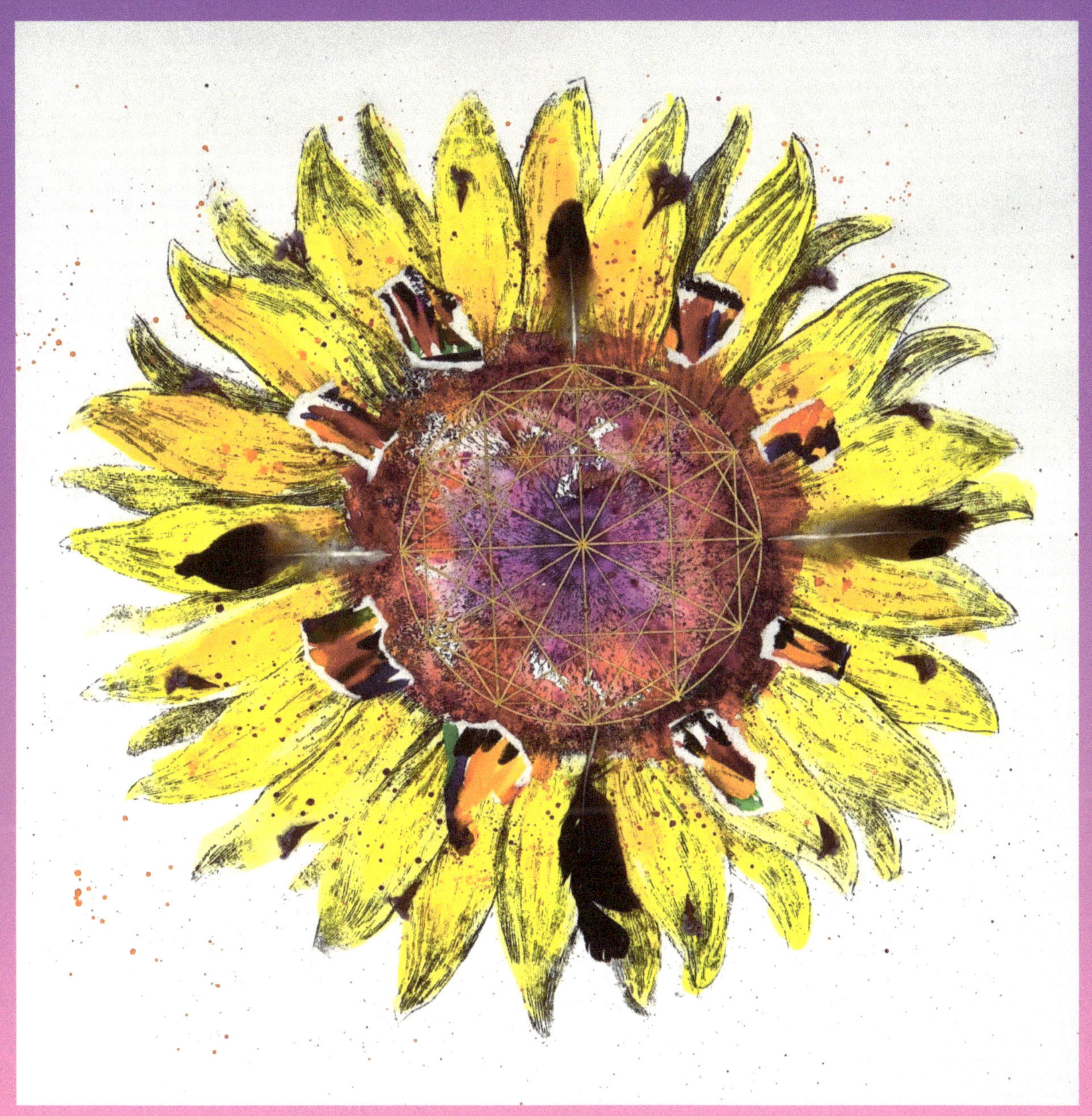

GOODNESS

COMING OUT

There is so much help
in the Cosmos.
As we emerge
and grow,
we are loved and protected
in unseen ways.
There is a grid of light
around all growing things
as they rise out of their holy seed.
My grandpa,
from the other side of time,
said "gladly" when I asked
him for help.
We have so much more
help than we realize.

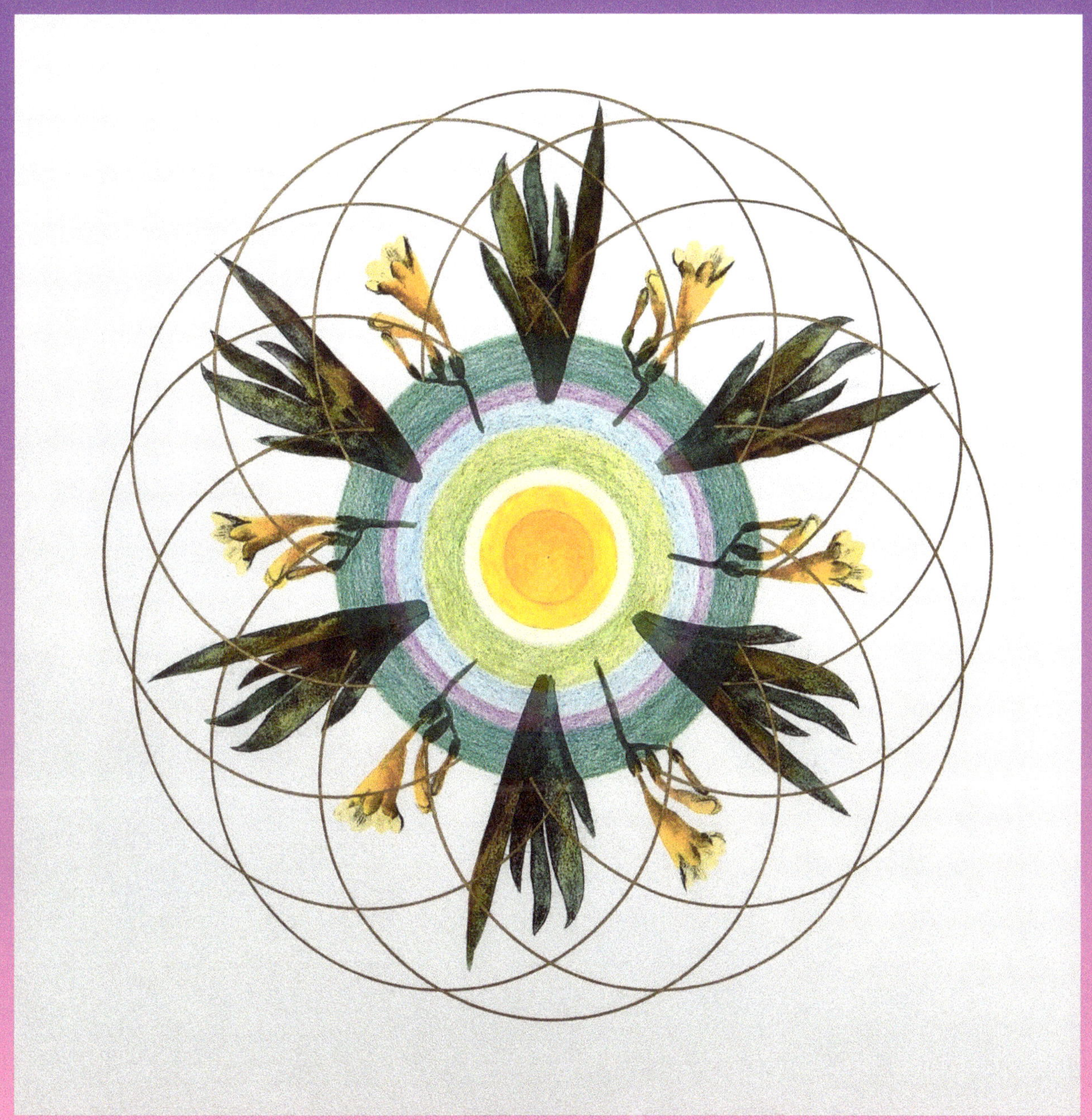

COMING OUT

BUDDING POTENTIAL

With each new sprout and blossom,
the Sun and the Moon and the Cosmos
infuse it with budding creativity,
calling it forth
in a swirl of love.
On this planet of boundless creativity,
with infinite energy,
and bursting with joy and excitement,
the Cosmos sprinkles us all,
with a fiery spark,
to ignite what is already living within.
All are blessed and
carry the magnificence of the Creator.
All are ready to crack wide open.
Can you see it?
Look within your heart.

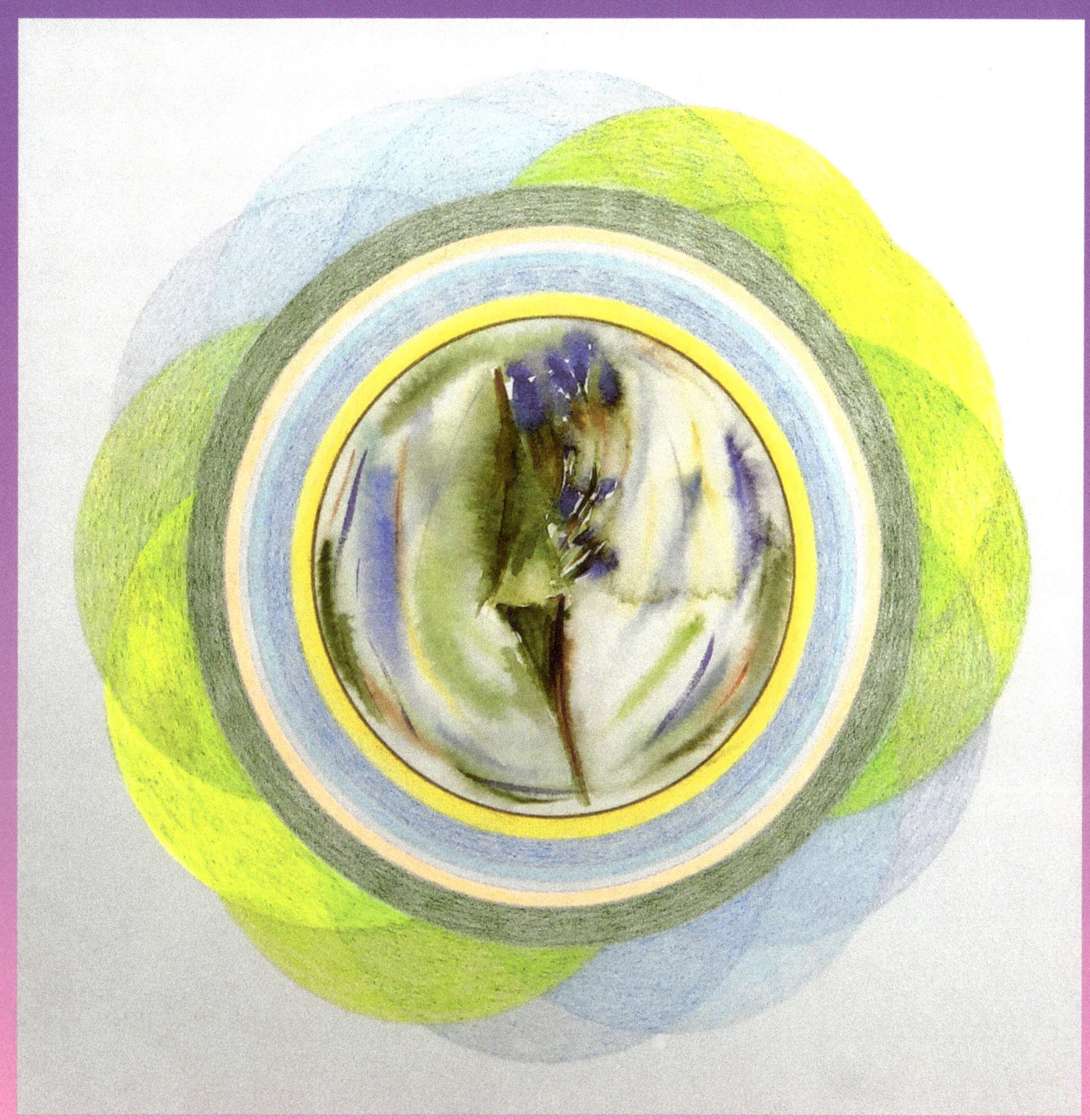

BUDDING POTENTIAL

BEING OK AND NOT WRONG

The sun warms
the quiet soil.
It is dark, rich, fertile
and it awaits, receptive.
There is unseen activity within,
there is unlimited possibility.
For the untrained eye
nothing is happening.
A sprout emerges,
it is curious.
What happens if I come up for air,
show myself,
and reach for the sunshine?
I am ready.
The flower says to her:
I will help you come through the darkness,
it's just part of the process of life,
the germination process.
Wanting to emerge to experience your fullness
is not wrong.
It is a natural urge to grow.
Look! You are more than OK!
How beautiful you are.

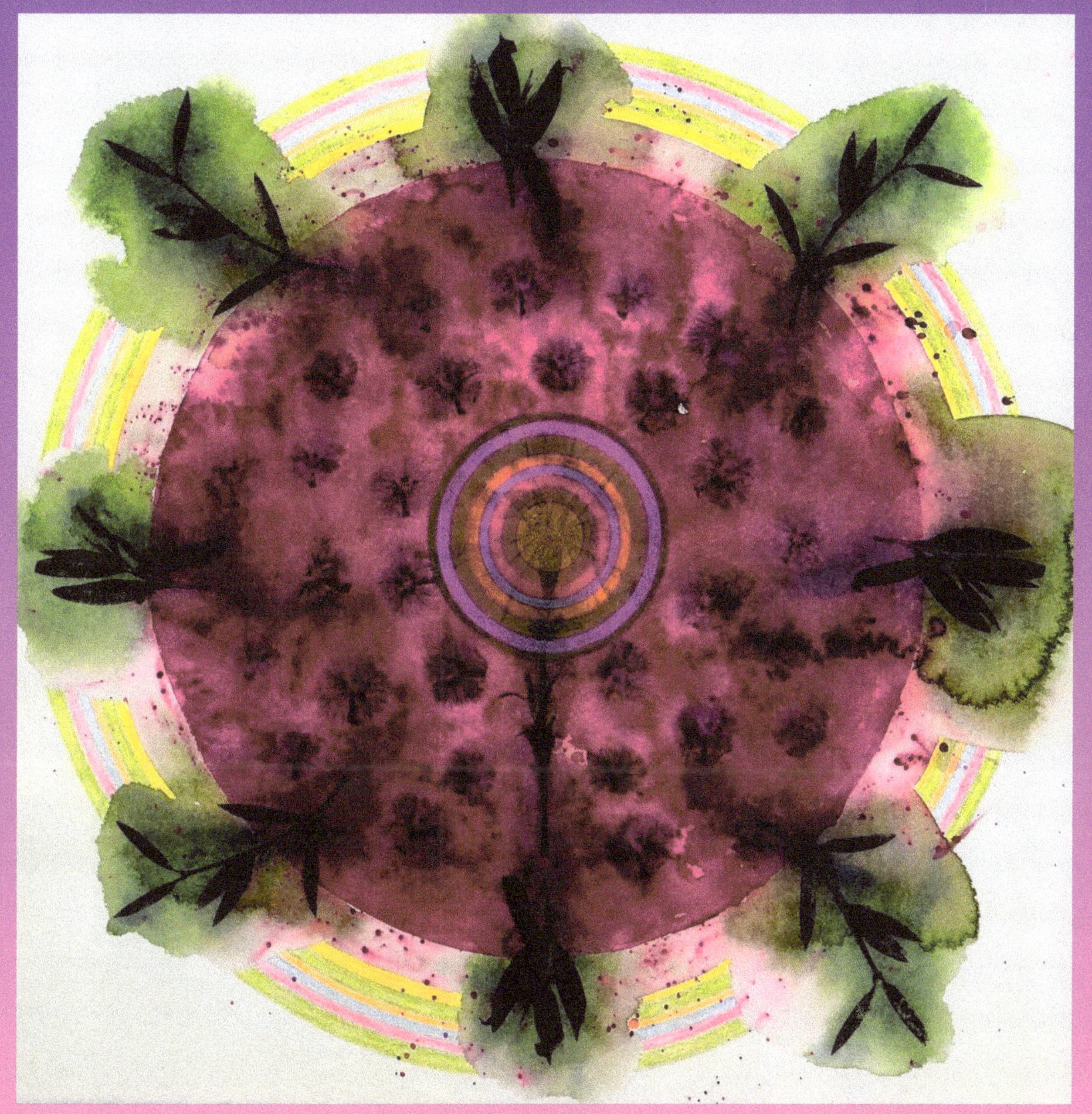

BEING OK

INTERNAL HELP

This internal Sacred Heart
is radiating and pouring forth love.
In a very blessed vision, I saw it
surrounded, protected and supported
by the Divine parts
of the Self
represented by the beautiful,
passionate poinsettias.
I am very drawn
to Sacred Hearts,
they are very comforting.
But in my
spiritual upbringing,
it wasn't one of our religious symbols.
How sad it was,
that in my youth
I had never seen one.
But once I did,
it became a deeply important
Divine presence for me.

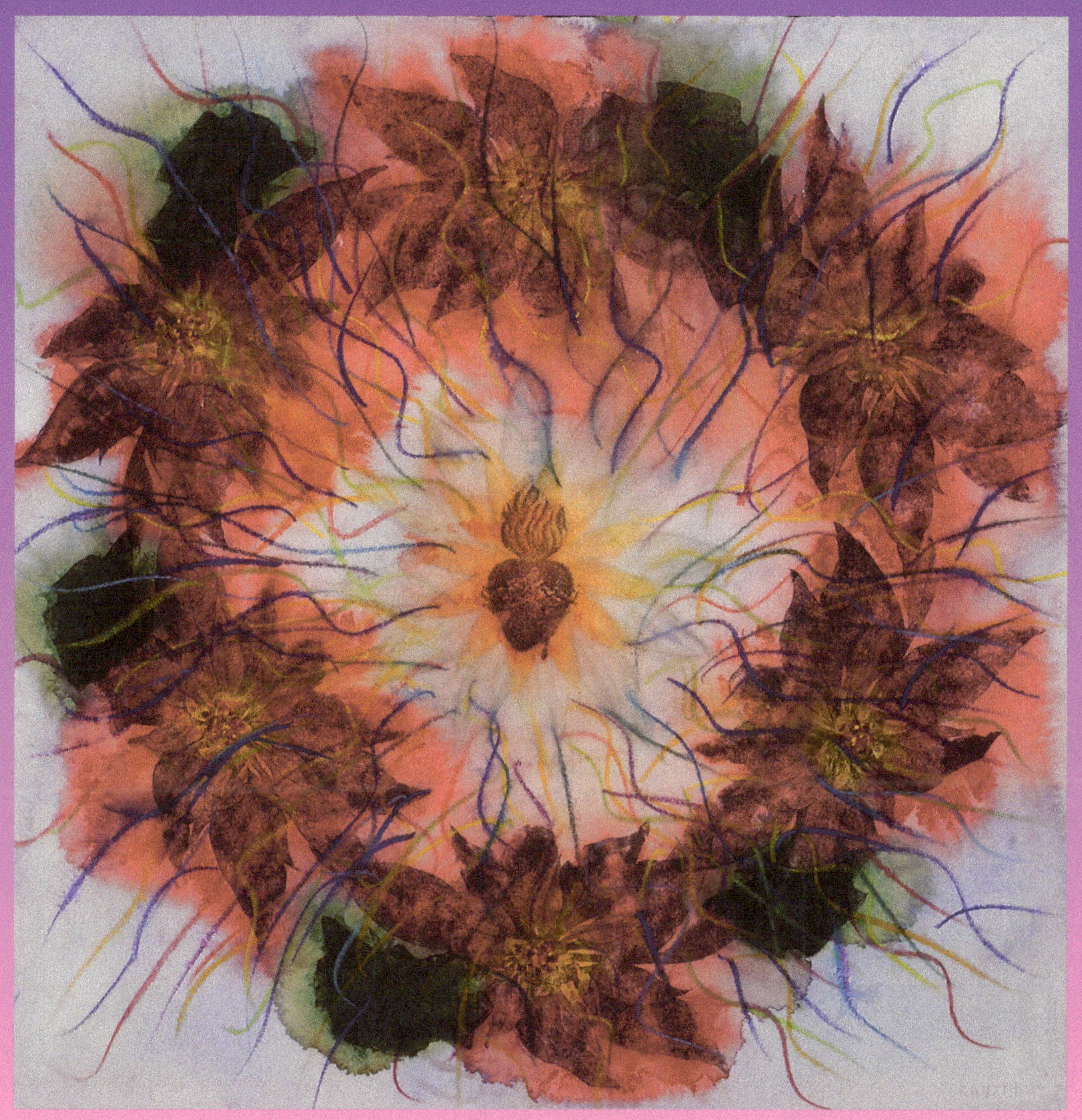

INTERNAL HELP

GOD AS HYDRANGEA

It came in a flash,
a vision of perfect, symmetrical beauty.
She was big and bright,
a luscious deep pink
and radiating from her heart center
were such consuming flames of love.
She, one flower made of many,
spoke to me in a language
of sweetness, caring and strength,
with a gentle voice
which I gave myself over to hear.
On a deep breath I listened.
It was a message
from the whole of the flower kingdom.
We are all faces of the Divine.

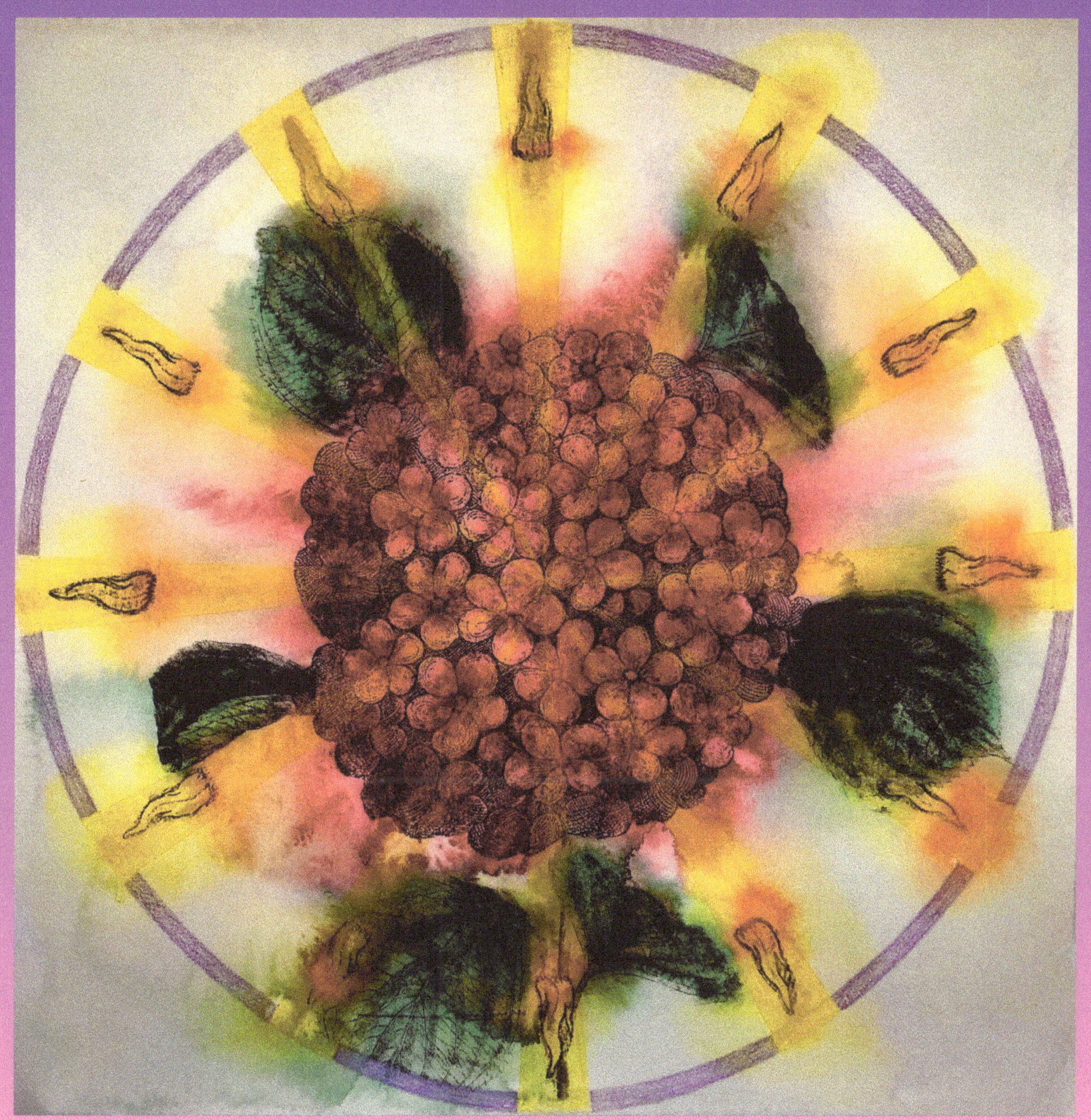

GOD AS HYDRANGEA

TWIG VISION

Creativity called,
from the Cosmos
and the dirt.
The twigs kept swirling
around my feet,
insisting that I create with them.
I scooped them up.
It was fun and playful
and I was excited.
"Finally," they said.
I giggled to myself.
Mandalas <u>are</u> everywhere.
Breathe in creativity from
the breath of the All.
Breathe out creation.
The universe wanted to play,
and that's where our creativity lives.
In play!
We are all children
at play in the universe.

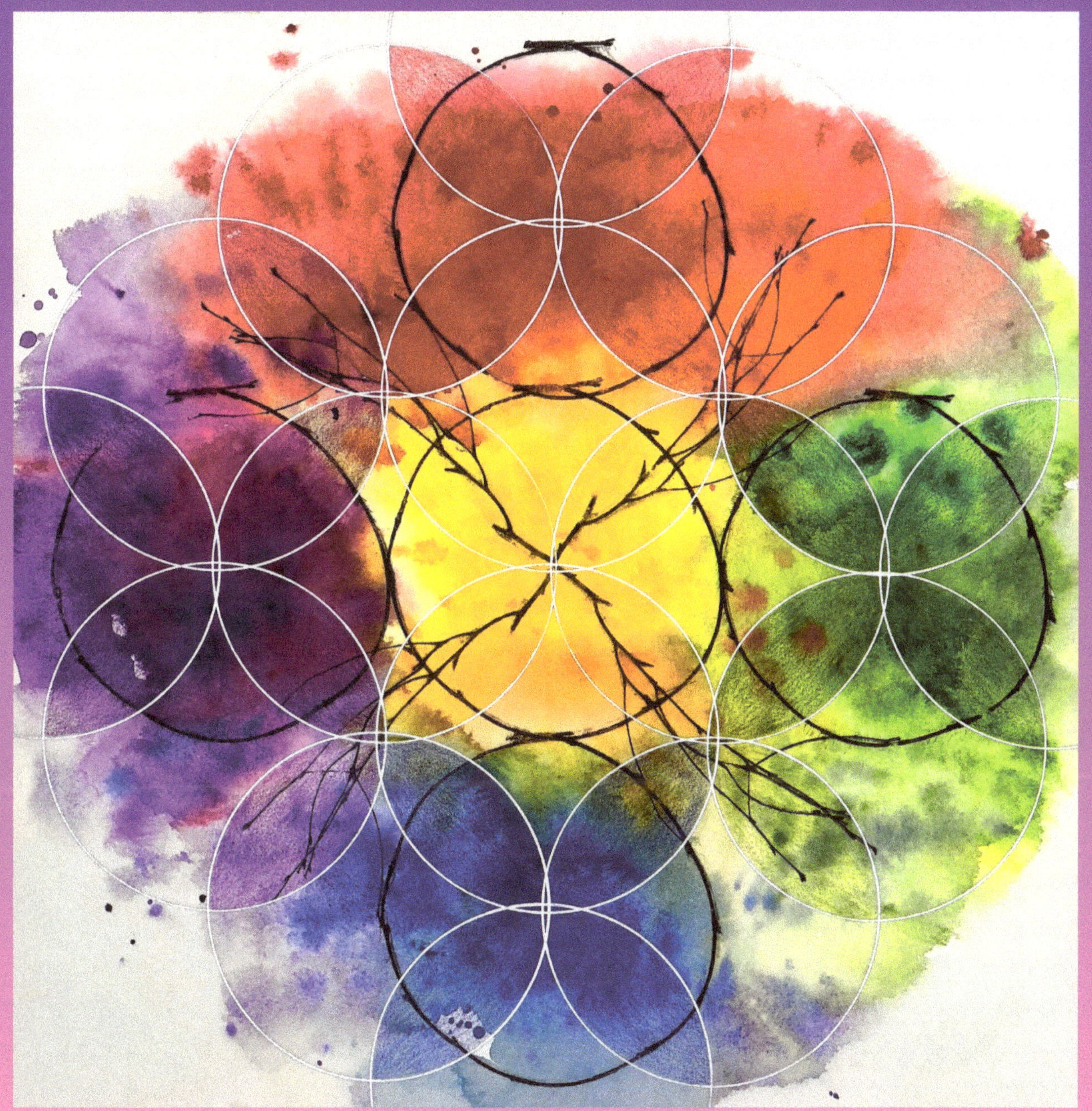

TWIG VISION

MY SACRED SELF CHILD WITHIN

You have a magnificent sacred inner child.
Take care of her,
encourage her to come forward
and be part of your Whole Divine Self.
She is a valuable part of you
and commands a rightful place.
She gives you a lot,
so give her space and place.
Honor her, and let her play.
She makes you whole
and is an essential part
of your Divine Self.
—From one of my spiritual teachers.
As my paint flowed,
these words followed in my mind
and I wrote them on the back of the painting.
She is:
deep, raw, passionate,
emotional, powerful, strong,
loving, playful, deeply feeling,
fleshy, celebratory, intense
and happy.

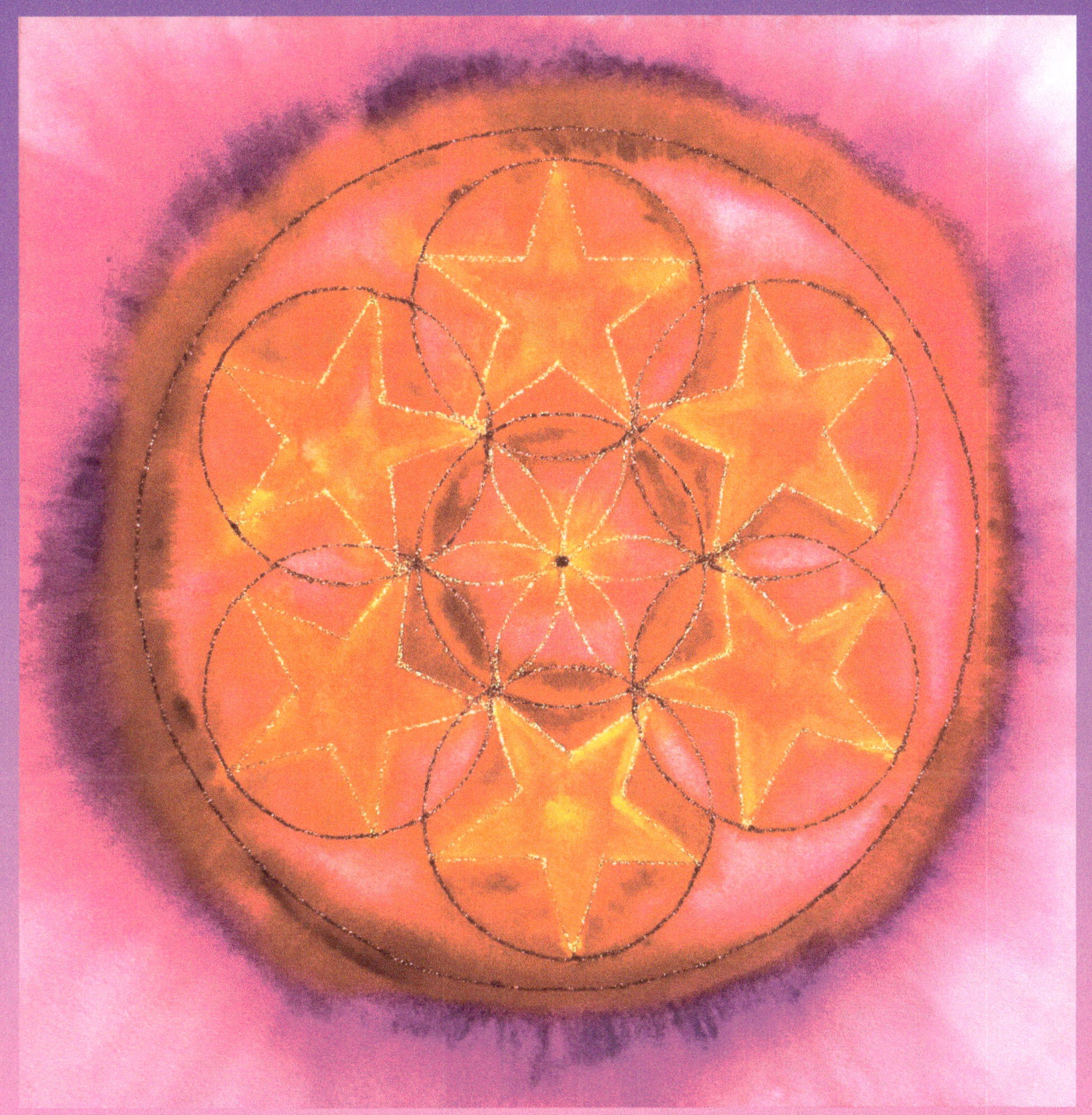

MY SACRED SELF CHILD WITHIN

FLIGHT OF THE SOUL

What is the dance of the universe?
We all have our own signature moves.
Our Sun and Moon,
the stars, planets and galaxies
have their cosmic revolutions.
I watch the earth's skies in summer
when I see the swallows return
for their encore performance.
I am energized by their dance,
the darting and diving around me,
and I catch my breath
when they barely miss me!
I am moved by
anyone's dance.
That energy touches me
like a bird's wing brushing my cheek.
I smile and want to join.
Aren't we all connected
in a swirling dance of energy,
not only with our feet
but our body, soul and spirit?
Imagine a world
with everyone smiling and
dancing their days.

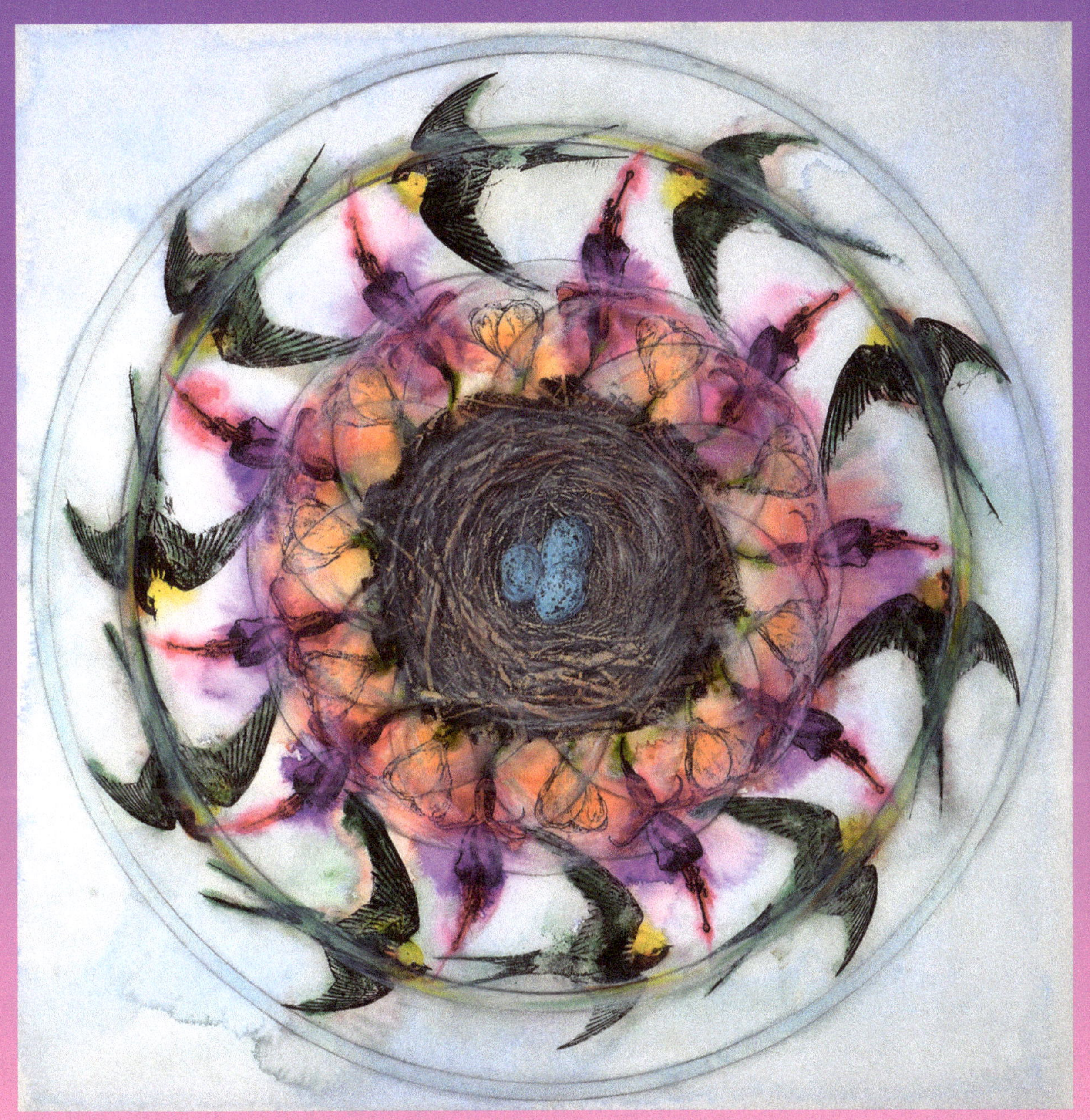

FLIGHT OF THE SOUL

NOURISHING BERRIES

Returning from the land of dreams,
I awoke seeing berries.
Nourishing blackberries.
Berries, I learned,
were used by native cultures to wash wounds.
Was I on a healing journey
as I slept?
My body silently nodded yes.
Up from the underground,
old wounds were being brought
to the surface for air and light.
A scab continues that process,
diligent, beautiful, a miracle,
focused on its mission of healing.
It was mysterious and unexpected,
the berries from the night,
but a Divine gift.
Anemone flowers hold mysteries about the night too,
discovered in their morning's rebirth in light.
The petals close as the darkness appears,
and re-open at dawn as the light reemerges.
They are a soothing reminder that
light follows after the darkness.

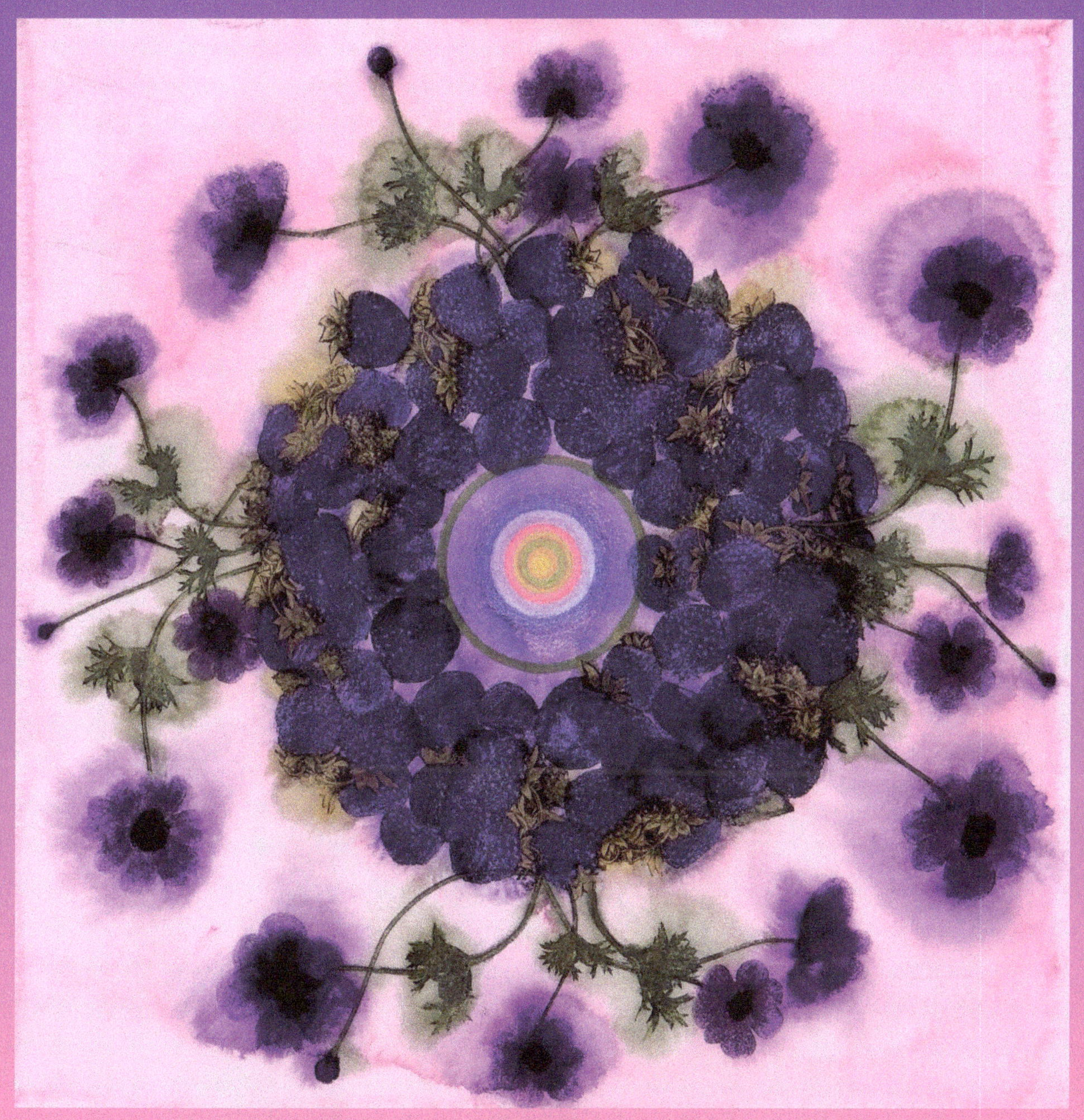

NOURISHING BERRIES AND NURTURING ANEMONES

CAMELLIA IS CARING

Have you ever been hugged by a flower?
Or had a flower talk to you?
I have come to believe that life is not complete,
until you've heard their beautiful whisper,
or felt their fragrant squeeze.
Did you know that all you have to do is ask,
and open your heart?
A few years ago I needed a message, and so I asked for one.
The word "caring" came in the middle of the night
along with the image of a red camellia.
I had forgotten I could do that.
Having been so focused on getting well,
with the challenge of cancer,
my communication with my higher Self
had taken a backseat.
This message was such a blessing
and opened the floodgates once again.
Recently the camellia
found her way into my heart again by hugging me.
Surprised and delighted,
by the Divine energy which wrapped itself around me,
I breathed in ecstasy and giggled to myself.
Oh, she wants to be in this book!
I am in awe of her holy purpose.
The beautiful camellia is caring,
and reminds us to be the same.

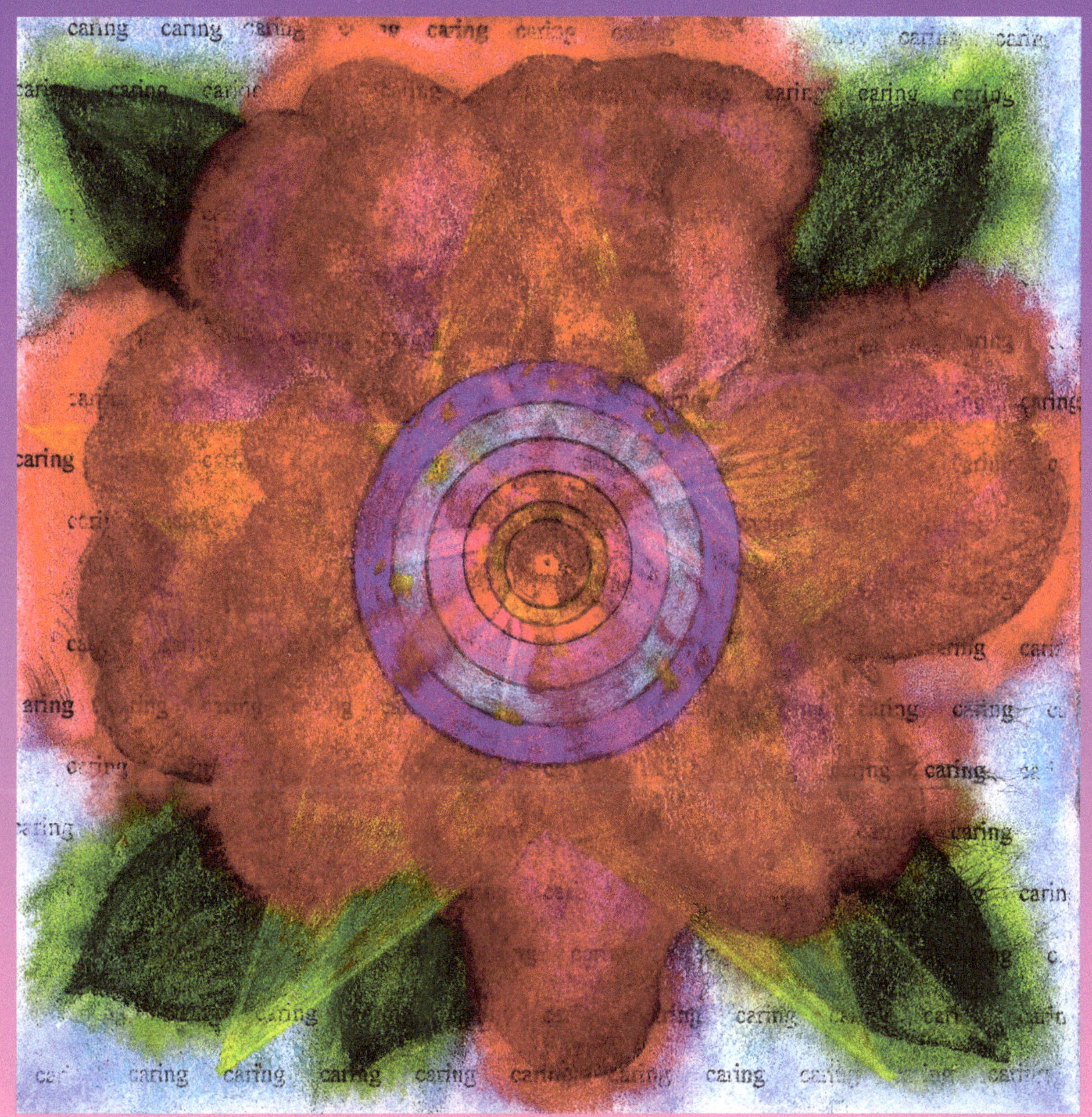

CAMELLIA IS CARING

DYING TO BE BORN ANEW

From the golden center within a precious egg,
a Divine spark of love begins to grow.
She smiles with anticipation.
She does not forget her connection to Spirit,
on her path of rebirth,
and holds the vision of becoming a lotus,
most prized among flowers.
She will get nourishment,
thriving from the mud and water below the surface,
and then will emerge quietly, but powerfully,
into another dimension,
to be welcomed by the light and air of the sun.
Dying to the old limited patterns of being,
she blossoms into her Divine Self,
and she is free and beautiful.

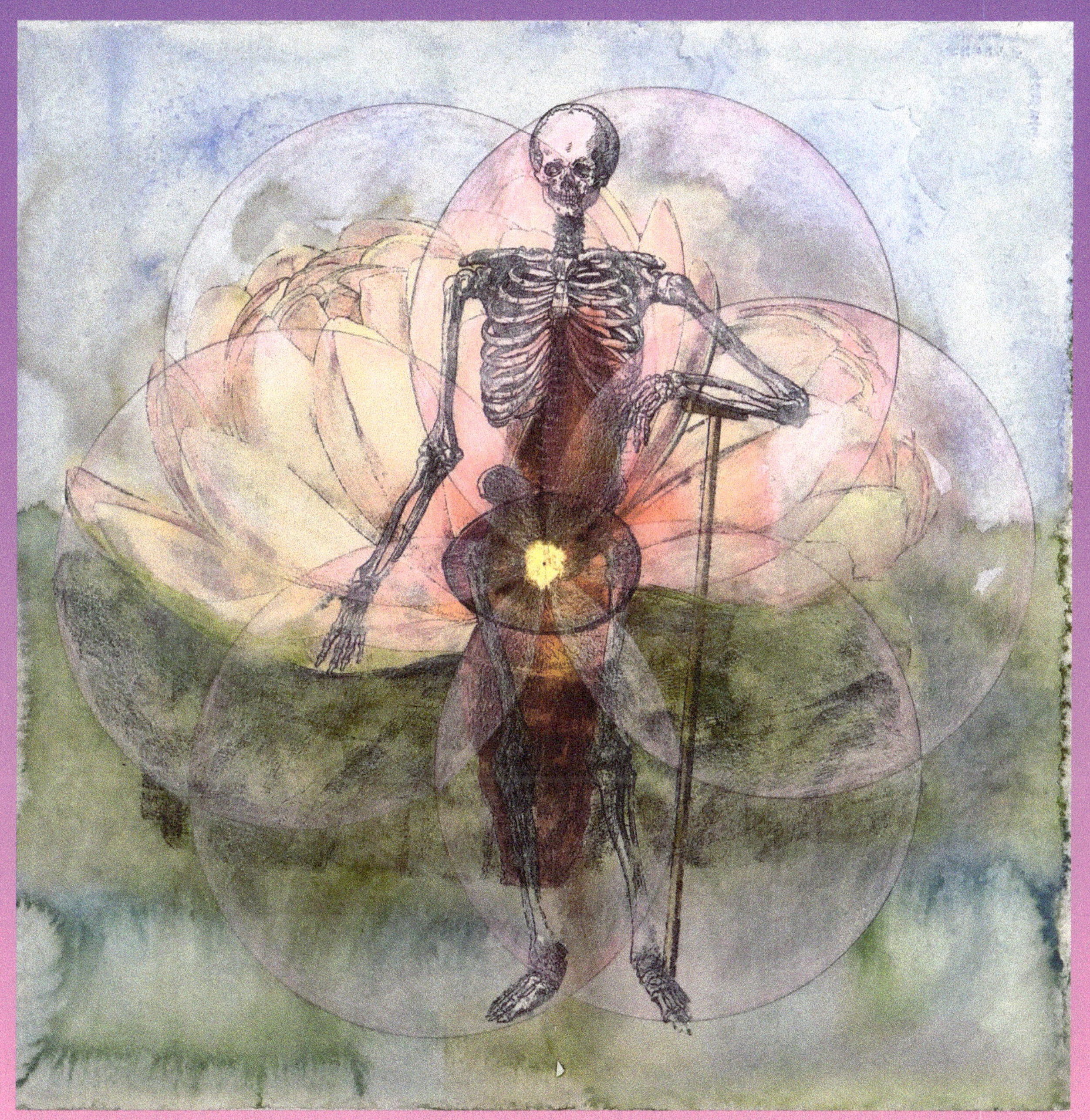

DYING TO BE BORN ANEW

SING MY SWEETNESS INTO BEING

What was the first flower
you remember as a child?
Never to be forgotten,
I first saw the beautiful flowering snowball
outside the window at my grandparents' ranch,
as I napped.
The flowers framed the landscape I witnessed,
of blue skies, green pastures and contented cows.
I loved those flowers,
and what they represented for me;
unconditional love, safety and that "all was well."
I remember when all that disappeared,
at the time my loved ones
took their rightful place as angels.
Today those flowers take me back to the days of wonder
where I was blessed with utter acceptance.
Mercifully, snowballs now keep
my beautiful and unforgettable memories alive.
The blessed flowers return each season,
and this year a bluebird alighted
on the pure white, fluffy blossoms.
What good fortune.
The flowers will inspire her to sing a melody
which will continue the good work
my grandparents began so long ago.
A song of Love.

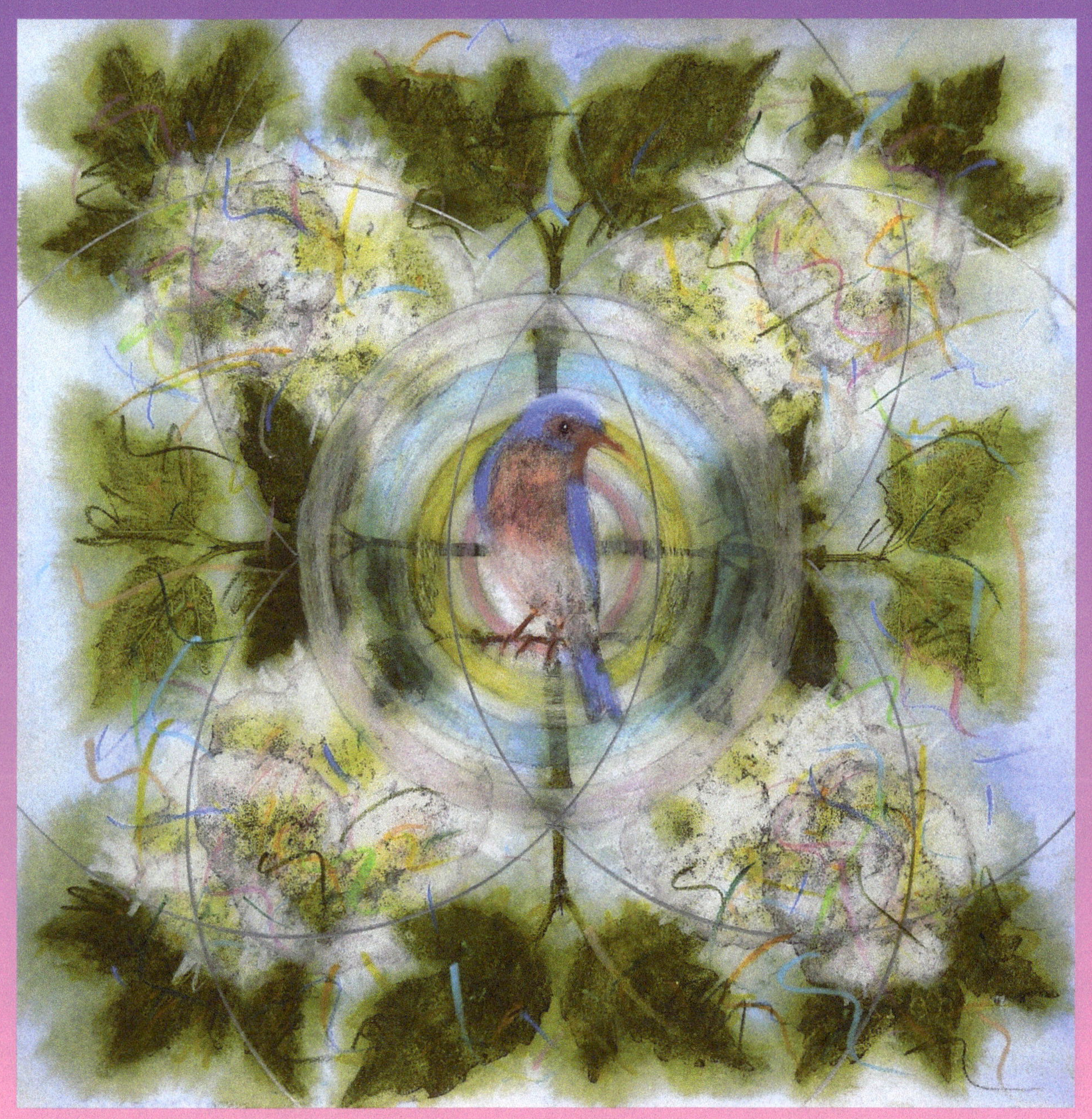

SNOWBALL, INSPIRE THE BLUEBIRD TO SING MY SWEETNESS INTO BEING

BURNING AWAY DEFEAT

Seeing tomato slices in flames,
and "flame" parrot tulips on fire,
was quite a vision!
I knew immediately its message was about strength;
the strength and power of the Self,
and its ability to overcome inner challenges
which could defeat and take me down.
These words rolled around in my head, playfully,
until I wrote them down:
"It's a feat
to defeat
defeat."
I have learned, and am still on that path,
that when one of those old voices raises
its sad and frightened heart,
I throw my arms around her,
and hug her with love, understanding and compassion,
until she understands
that flames of love
purify and heal everything.

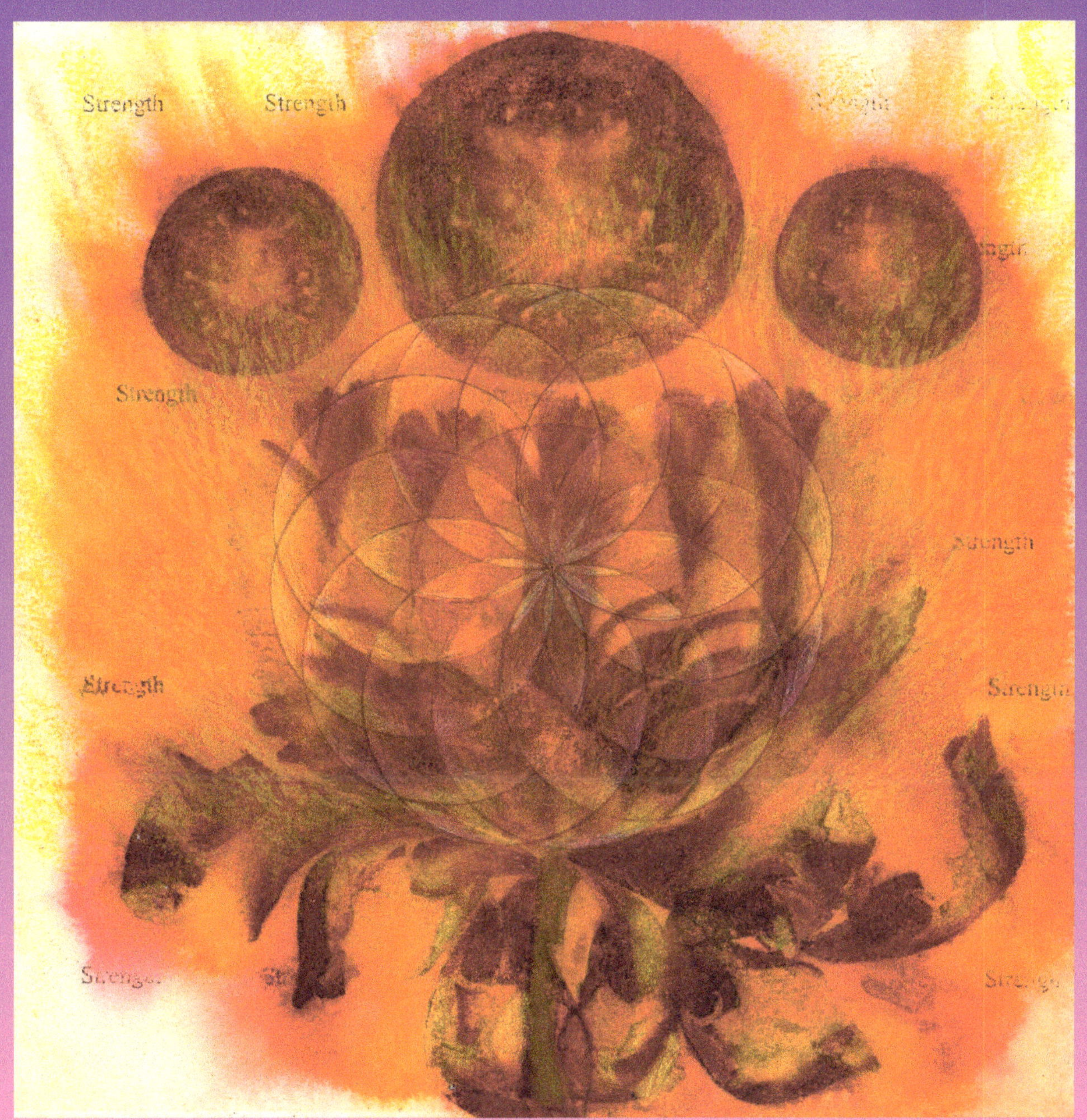

BURNING AWAY DEFEAT

GO FOR IT

You touched me with your loveliness,
your sweet, soft power,
in a beautiful vision I had of white callas
brushed with pink.
They are flowers of the Goddess.
Her message was clear:
Life: lift yourself up to it,
resurrect, go for it, stand up.
From the high reaches of that Divine voice,
I heard it and let it fill me.
With it came courage
to stand tall and project light,
to live my life more fully connected
and spiritually committed.
With support such as this,
I knew that I had the strength and power
to live my higher purpose and succeed.
Who would bring such a call
for sacred resurrection
with so much beauty, tenderness
and strong, loving care?
The one source,
the Goddess of Flowers,
the Divine Feminine.

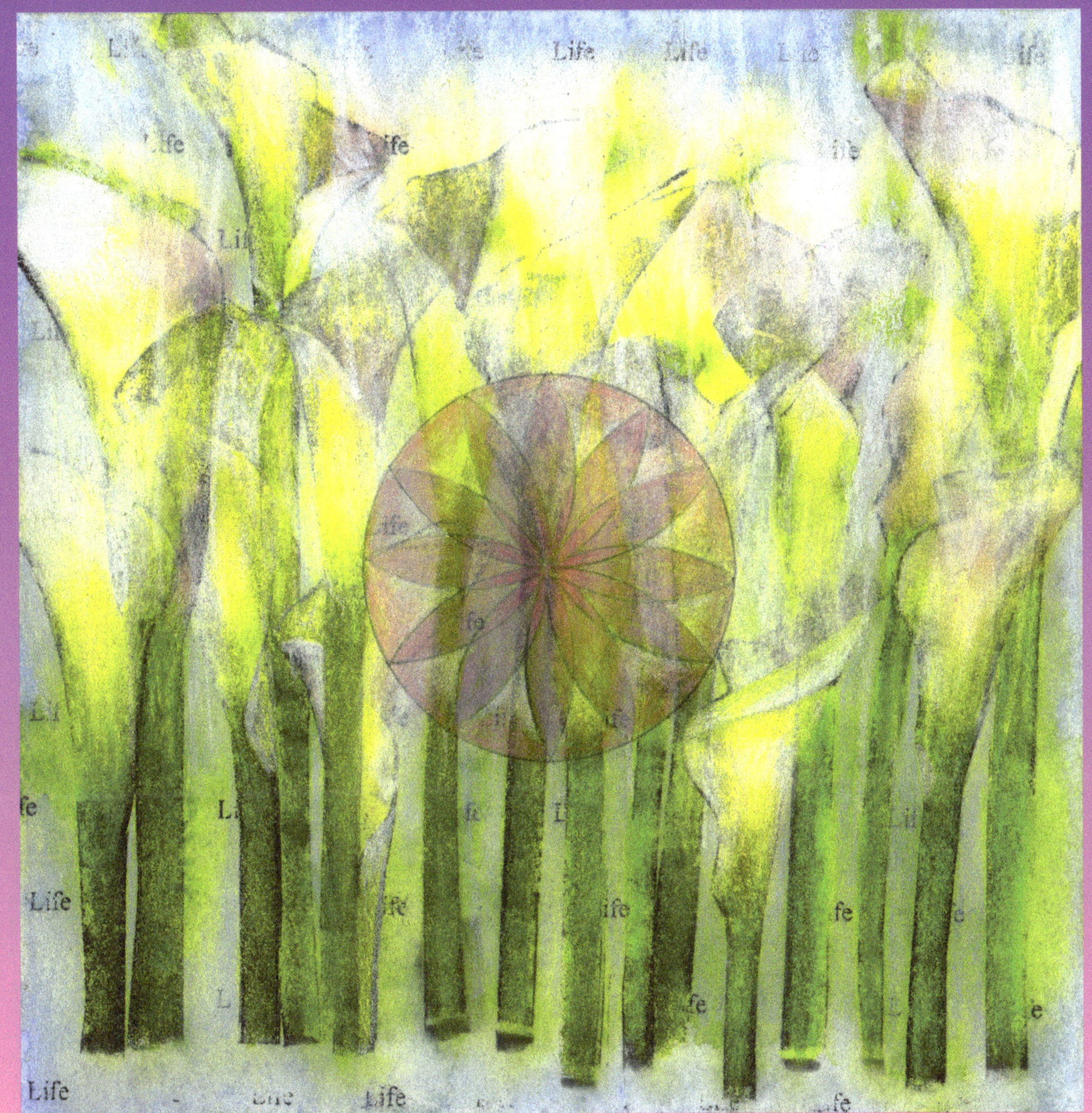

GO FOR IT

STEP OUT OF THE DARKNESS

This image drew me in
and these words completed the vision,
as I awoke from my nighttime slumber:
Step out of the darkness
and into the limelight.
I knew it was a signal to open the portal
and walk into the successes which awaited.
Could I accept and welcome this invitation?
Or was it one of those universal conditions
which speaks too quietly for anyone to hear
except our own shy and tender hearts?
"No I can't; I'm not good enough,"
say the inner voices.
How many of the grandest intentions
have been slain by the dragon inside?
How many successes are foiled
for lack of making it to the light of day,
never mind the limelight?
I daresay it is time for action.
Gather the leaves of your glory
and make a crown.
It will suit you perfectly.
Do not delay, the world needs it.
Step forward crowned in light,
your light, which will never go out.
I am ready. Join me.

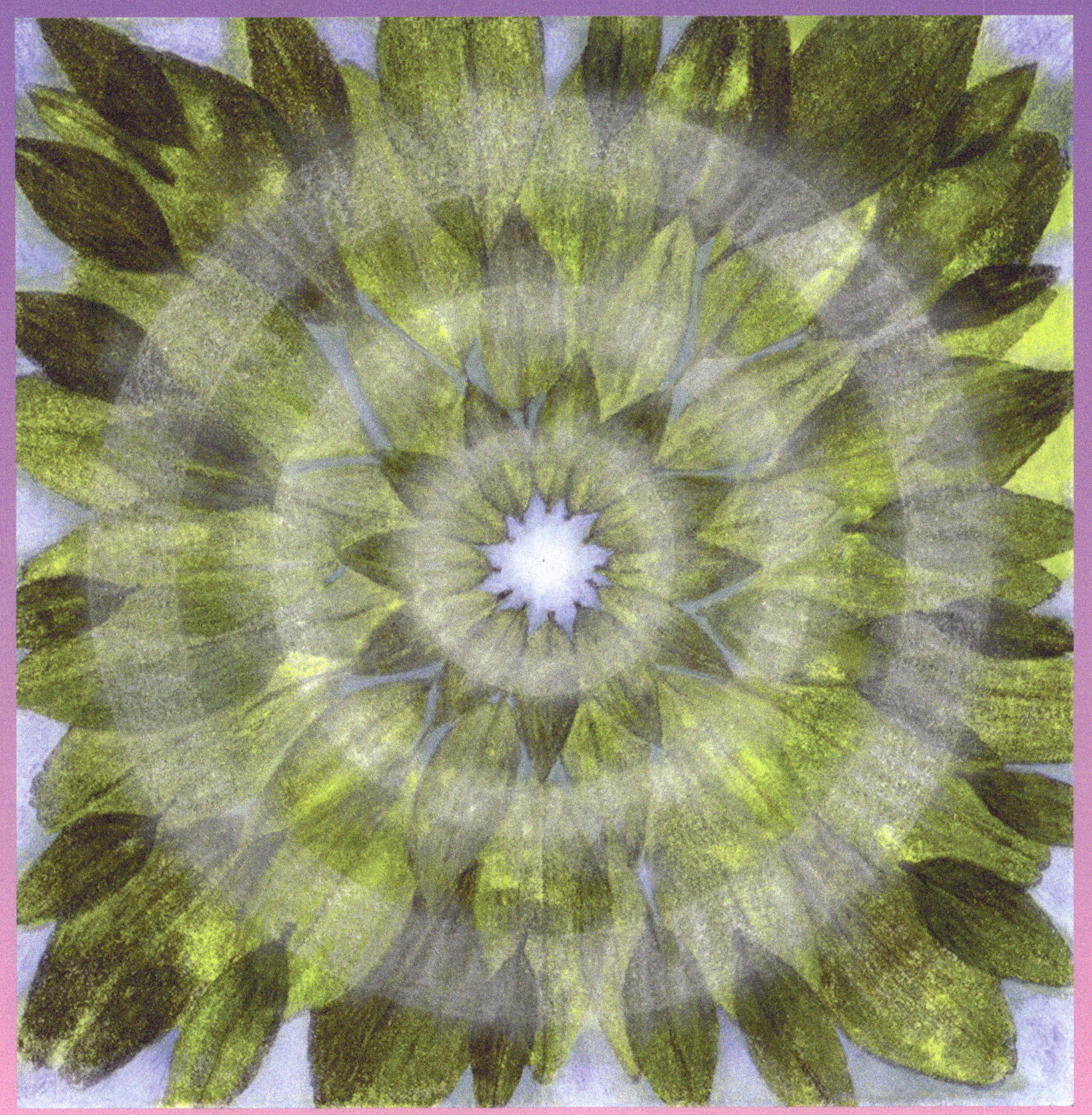

STEP OUT OF THE DARKNESS AND INTO THE LIMELIGHT

FIRST CHAKRA CIRCLE OF LOVE

Circle of Love,
I can hold you in my hands,
and bring you close to my heart,
as I ask for Divine assistance.
That was my intention inscribed on the back
of this self-made sacred object,
precious to me alone.
"Healing Spirit,
work with me in healing
my blood and bones –
flowing light up my spine
from Mother Earth,
so that I may be in perfect balance and health
and joyfully free of all dis-ease."
I am receiving the love and caring,
and the healing energies I asked for,
which flow so freely and powerfully.
I am being made whole.
Breathing deeply,
I am renewed with Holy breath

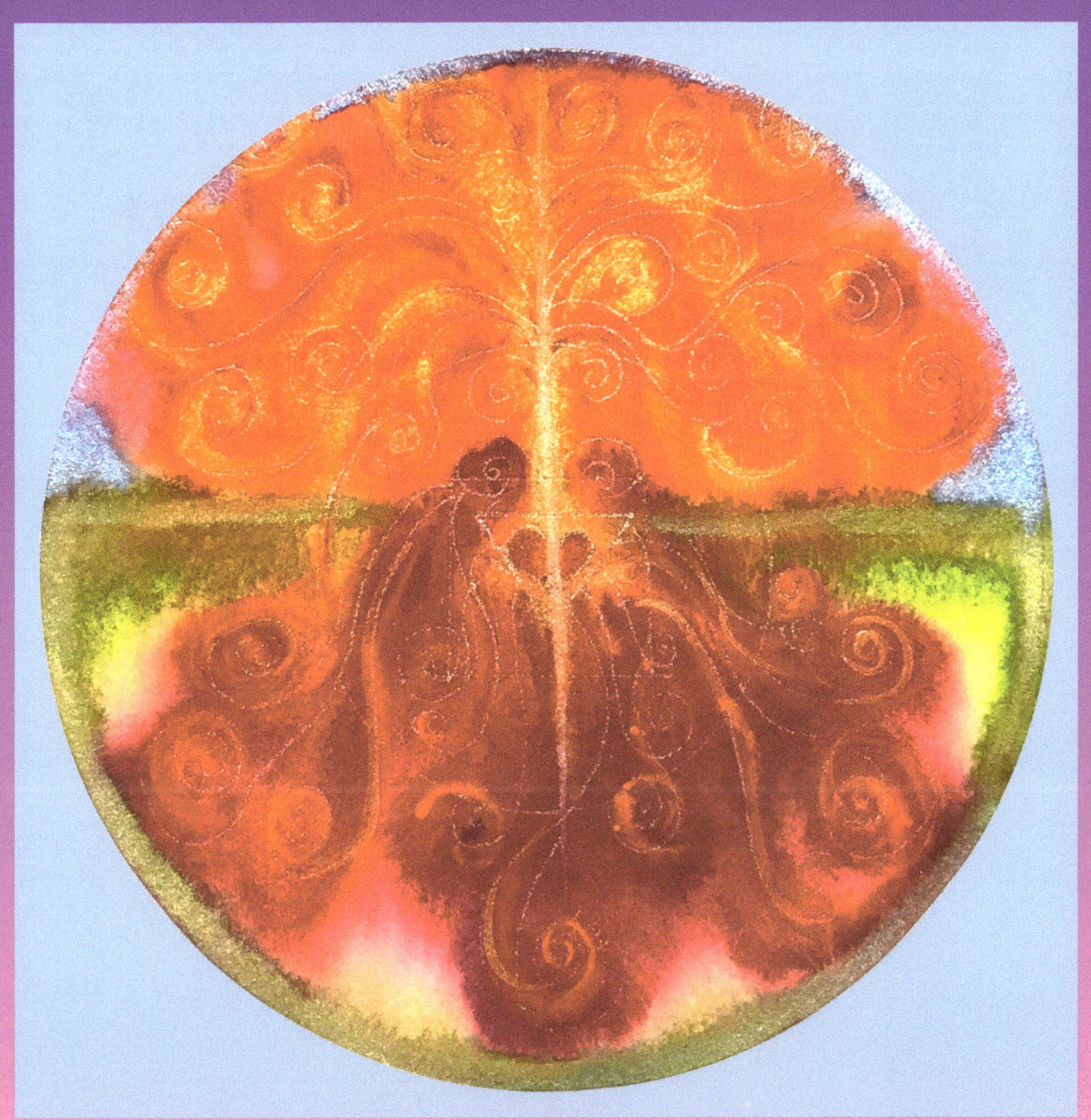

FIRST CHAKRA CIRCLE OF LOVE

NURTURING TURTLE

She brought me the gift of Animal Medicine,
this beautiful one.
I could feel where she made her home,
it was in my solar plexus,
where I had held my wounded feelings.
First appearing as a snapping turtle,
she was there to protect me,
creating a grid of sacred space for me
to go within and find my strength and heal.
She had been nurturing me for a long time,
in a sweet, caring and tender way.
What a gift she gave me,
of safety, of healing, of encouragement.
Surprising me now, she wanted
to come out and play.
A new adventure was on the horizon for us.
My depth of gratitude is boundless.
My thanks come by acknowledging
and honoring her, attempting to capture
her power in my recreation of the vision
I had of her when she arrived.
I created her as the Mother of all turtles,
and she is a symbolic mother in my world.

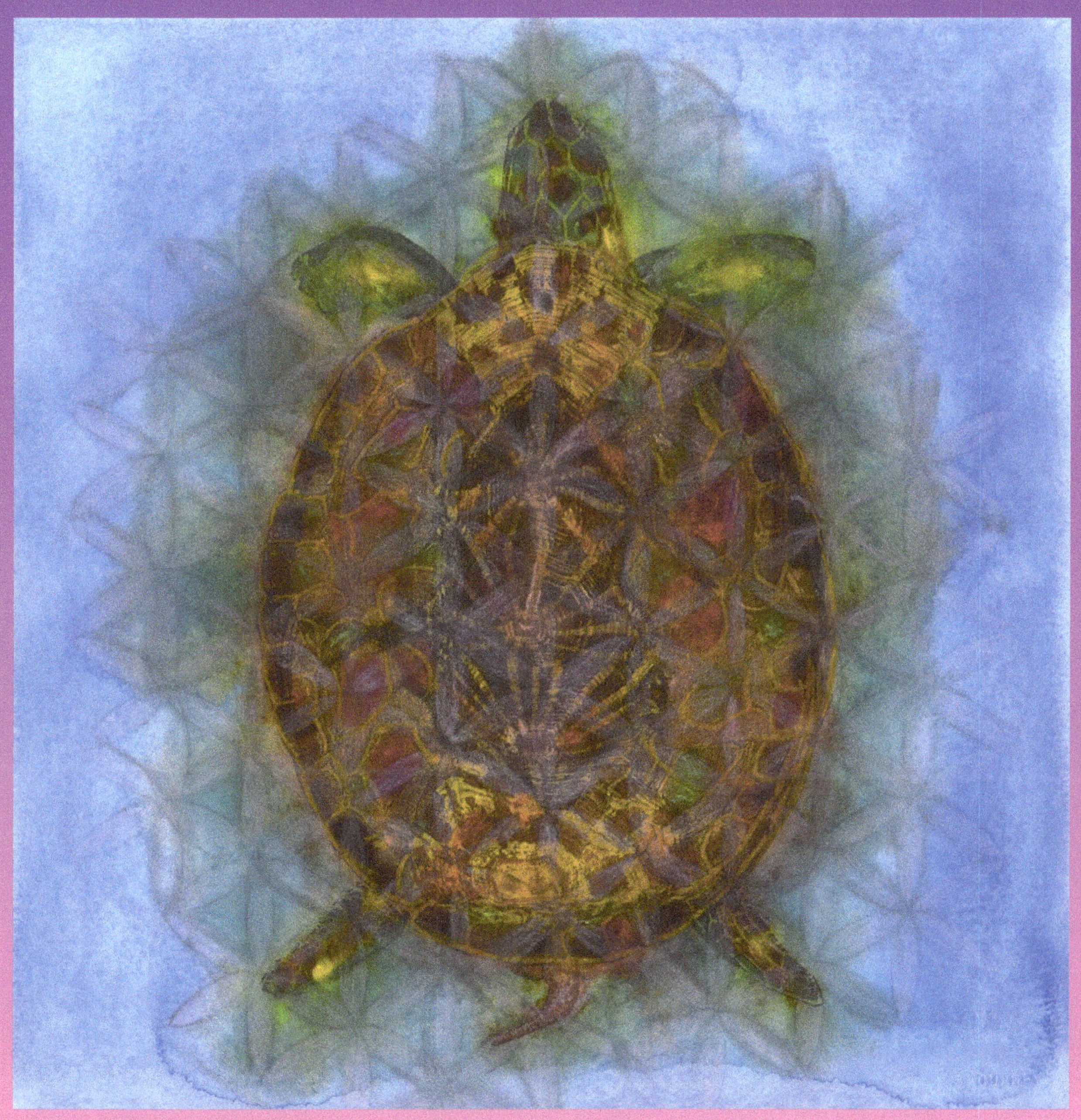

NURTURING TURTLE

GRATITUDE

The road to joy and happiness
is paved with gratitude.
The miracle of this is that it multiplies.
The more grateful we become,
the more we find to be grateful for.
And the more blessed we feel,
the more that love grows within us,
until we become grateful for everything.
Gratitude changes our life. It opens our heart.
It grows and multiples until
we become grateful not only for ourself,
but for everyone.
This painting began as a way
to express gratitude for my connection to Spirit,
for the spiritual guidance I receive,
and for the peace and beauty I feel
in connecting with nature.
The images representing my gratefulness,
the leaves and flowers,
surround the Flower of Life, the sacred geometry at the center.
Symbolizing the connection to Spirit,
the very ancient Flower of Life
also represents the connection we all have
to each other through Spirit.
It's a beautiful thing, gratefulness.
We are all blessed by it.

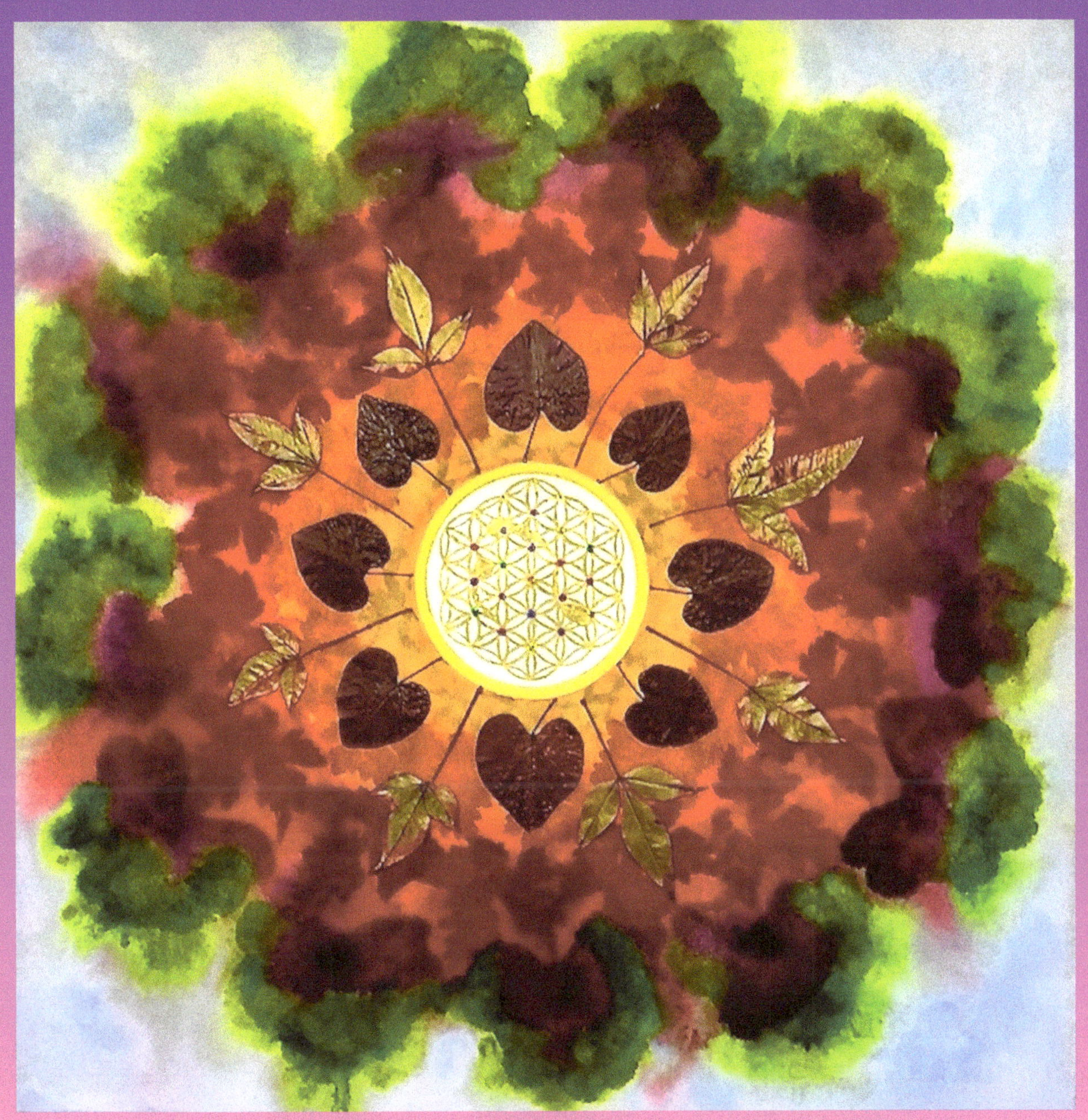

GRATITUDE

BLOOM! YOU ARE FREE

The star cried out,
"Bloom! And then you'll be free."
Oh, how wonderful to be supported
by a laurel of flowers created by our fellow stars.
The ones in our lives who surround us,
lift us up, give us courage,
and make a fairy ring of roses around us.
We are all stars shining brightly,
and blooming in our own rhythm.
Flowers we are, everyone of us,
fragrant, unique, colorful,
smiling and shimmering in the sunlight.
Such a gift to anyone
who stops in their rush,
and is receptive to the full import
of a unique blossom in full bloom.
Bloom! You are free.
Take your place among the stars.

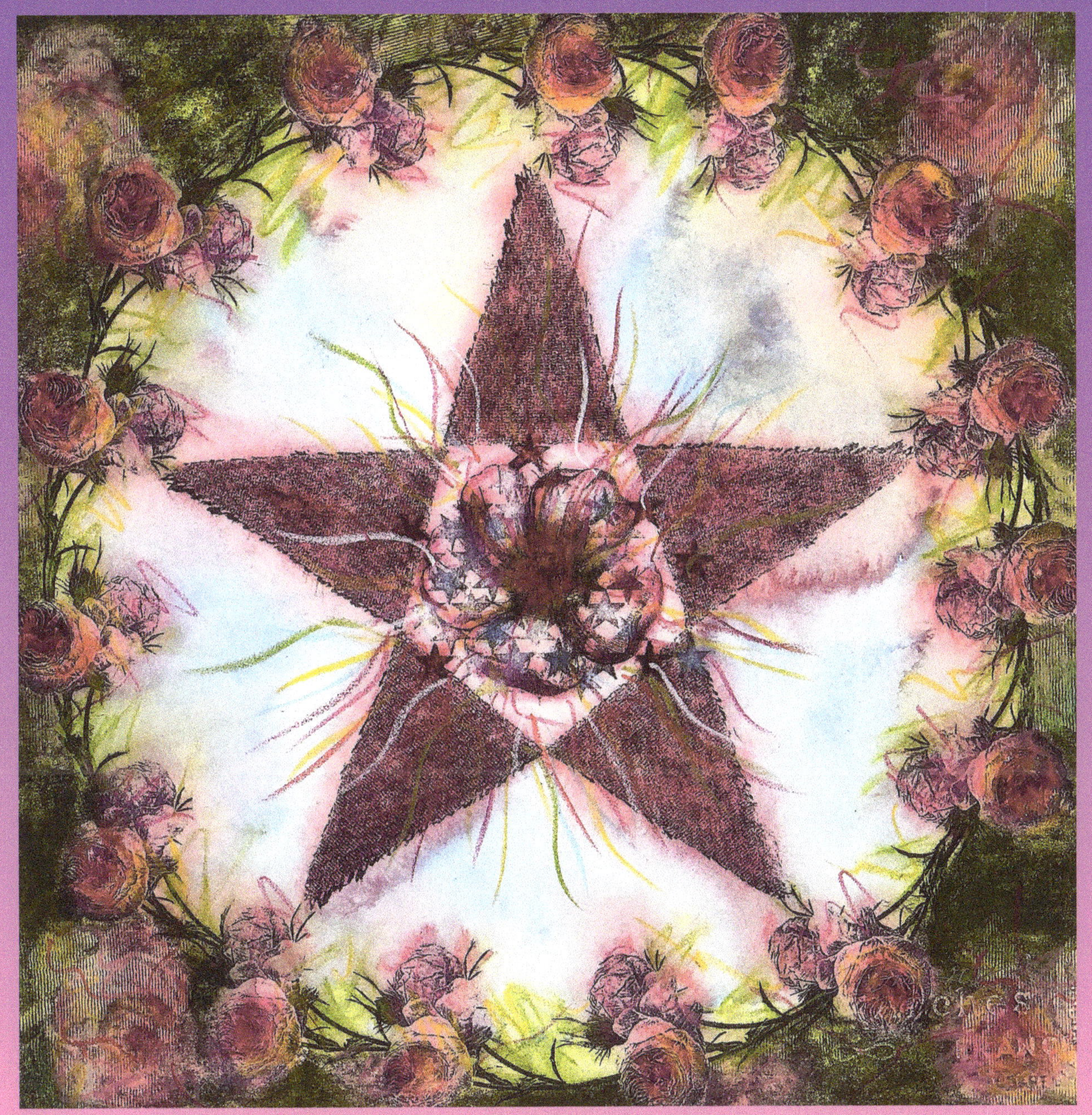

BLOOM! YOU ARE FREE

TRANSFORMATION

Life is about transformation
from one form of reality to another.
We all transform in our life.
From birth to death,
life is a series of changes.
How we transform is different for everyone.
But there is an ongoing evolution on this planet,
which started before we began walking upright.
Our bodies changed, our brains evolved.
Transformation is going on within us everyday.
The way is clear to me.
It's love that changes everything.
In this land of freedom, I am finding
my way home, where my heart is,
where I am loving more and fearing less.
Traveling into my ever-deepening heart,
I am breaking free from the binds of ancient patterns.
Bravely I am honoring my ancestors
who got me this far.
Loving and protecting my progeny,
I guide them so that they may step
fearlessly into their own higher calling.
I AM from the Home of the Brave.
I will wear my star proudly.

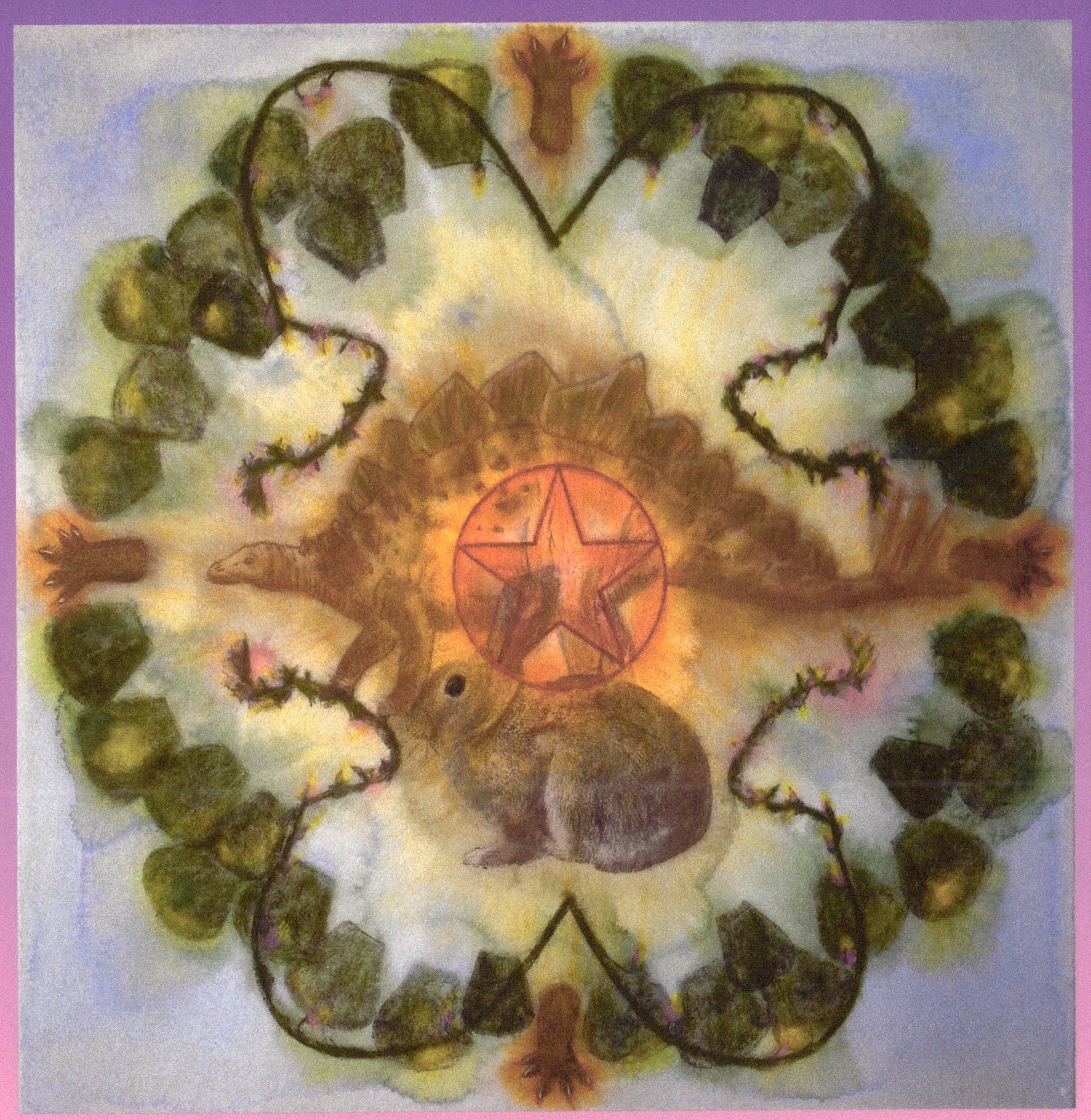

TRANSFORMATION: IN THE LAND OF THE FREE & HOME OF THE BRAVE

HEALING WITH ROSES

I had never seen the rabbits on my daily walks,
but they had always been there.
After I got this vision,
I delight in seeing them now,
and sometimes they don't run away.
This mandala is representative of the journey of healing.
Using the color, beauty, and energy
of roses from my garden,
the bunny is overlaid with a geometric pattern,
which itself is like a blooming flower.
Thinking about my vision,
the cottontail rabbit was a reflection
of the softness and vulnerability
of the inner self, my inner self.
That part of me used to hide, out of fear.
But the focus in this mandala is at the center,
where there is readiness to come out and to bloom.
I have practiced coming out of hiding,
of being myself and letting down my guard,
of being vulnerable, tender and soft,
and letting that bloom.
It is said that a rose is not a rose without the thorns.
If there were any thorns in my roses,
they were from a time long ago,
and my story now is a story of healing.

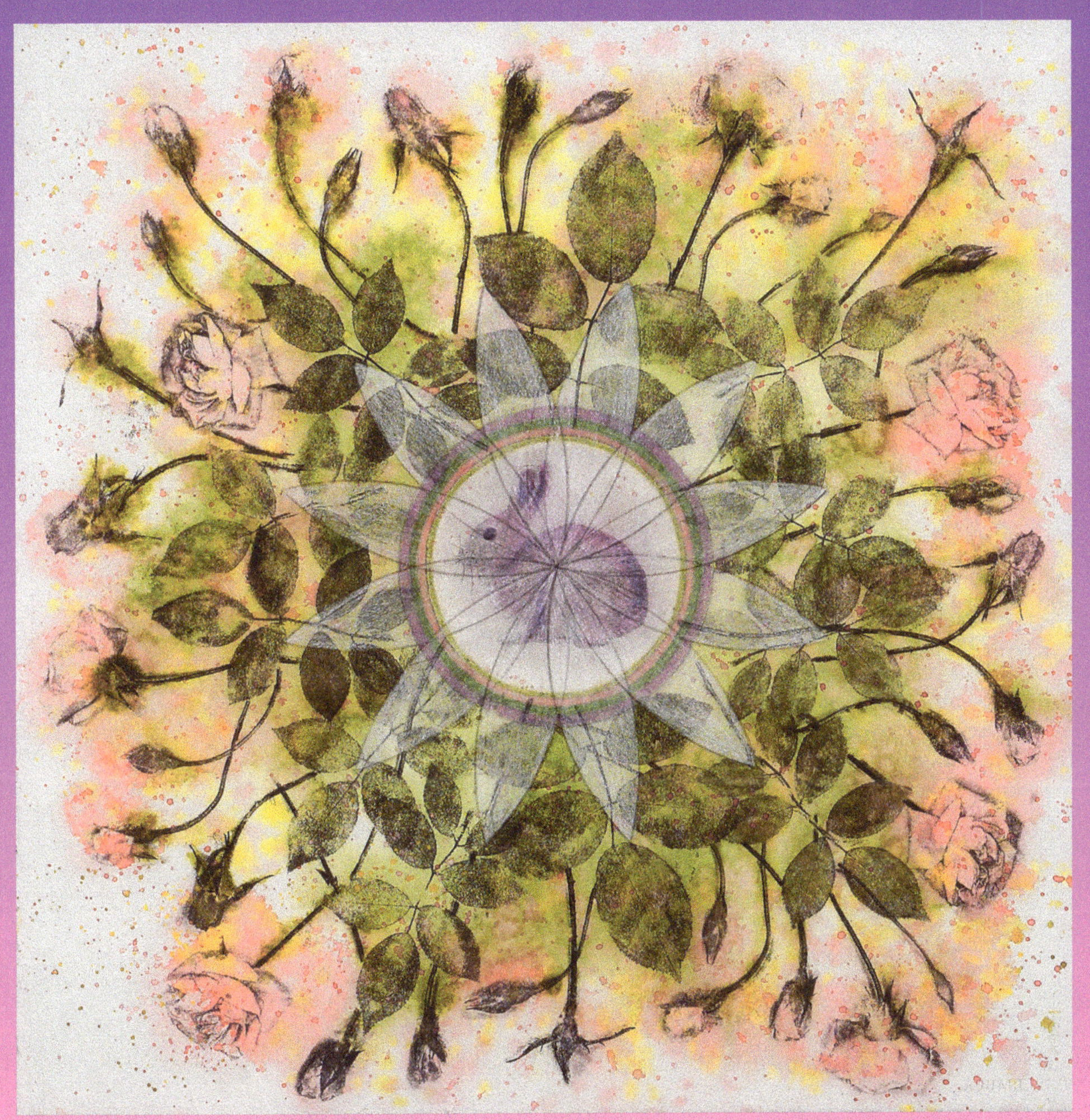

HEALING WITH ROSES; LOOKING TO SEE WHO I REALLY AM

THE HEALING FROM THE BROMELIAD

Free flowing blossoms overlaid with sacred geometry,
emanate a spiritual light.
Little and unique, the electric violet flowers
on the strong scarlet stems are beautiful,
and bloom again and again, almost unexpectedly.
Impossible to hold back, they keep blooming.
That small, bright flower
is like the little flower inside of ourselves.
With love, it blooms and blooms and blooms!
The bromeliad reminds us all,
to love and believe in ourselves.
Our beauty, our essence, our brightness and spirit,
is who we really are.
Connected to our heart, our uniqueness will bloom,
and like a flower,
be the gift to the world
we came to be.

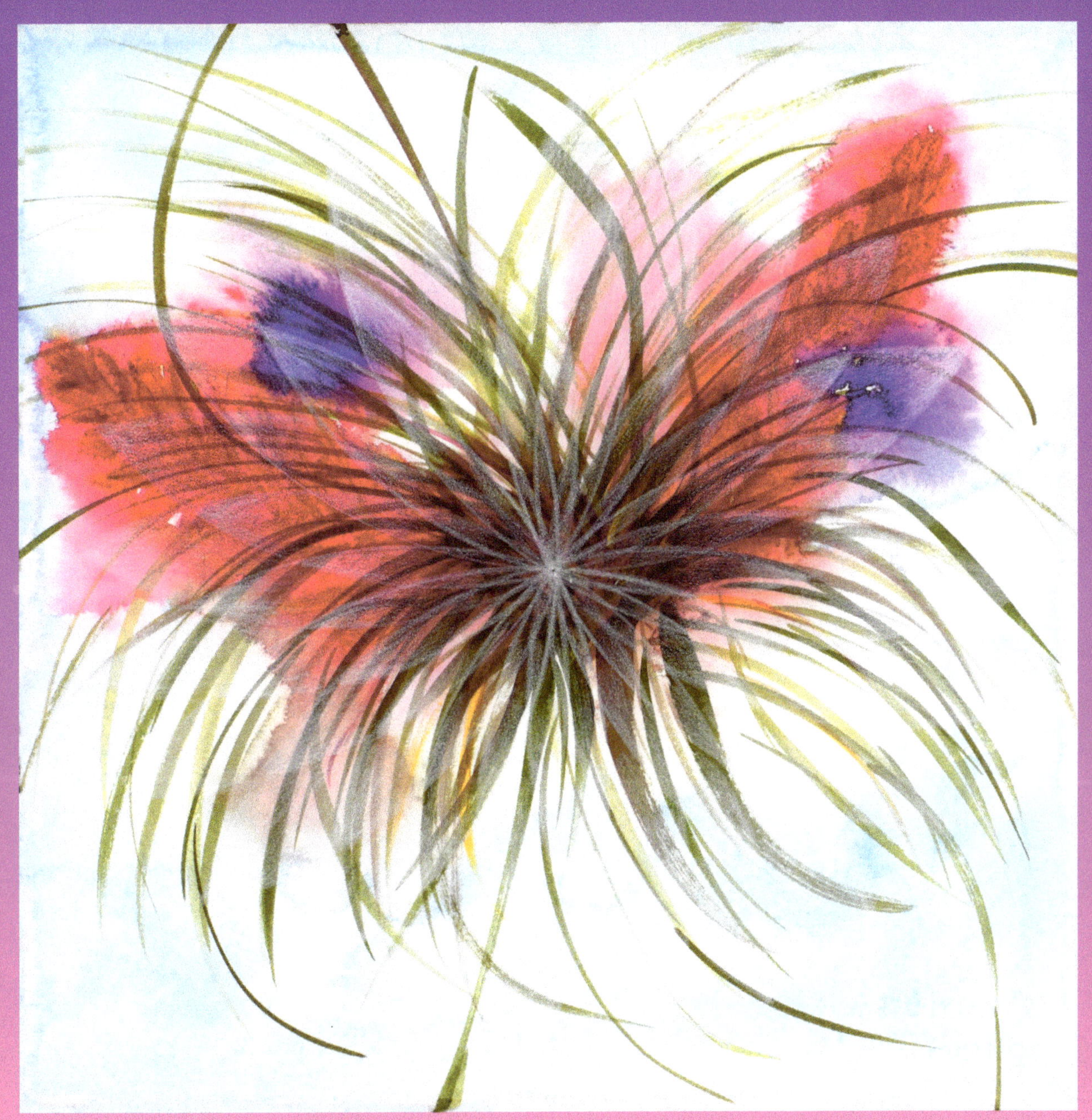

THE HEALING FROM THE BROMELIAD

CYCLAMENS COMING OUT OF A BIG HEART

Do you collect heart rocks?
Years ago I spotted one,
and now I'm always on the lookout
for another treasured heart.
It's a sweet thing, don't you think,
picking up a rock in the shape of a heart?
I have lots of them now,
and I love them.
They are alive and vibrate
a message of love to me.
I carefully placed one on the copier and enlarged it.
I had plans for it.
I wanted it for a vase for flowers in my mandala.
It made a perfect container for my cyclamens,
those flowers that look like shooting stars
with their petals reaching to the sky.
Oh, what a heavenly fragrance
the pink ones have too,
it carries me away into the realm of the Divine.
The vibrations which emanate light
from the center of the rock vase,
also transport me.
As solid as a rock,
and as ethereal as light is,
they make a beautiful bouquet
of Light and Love.

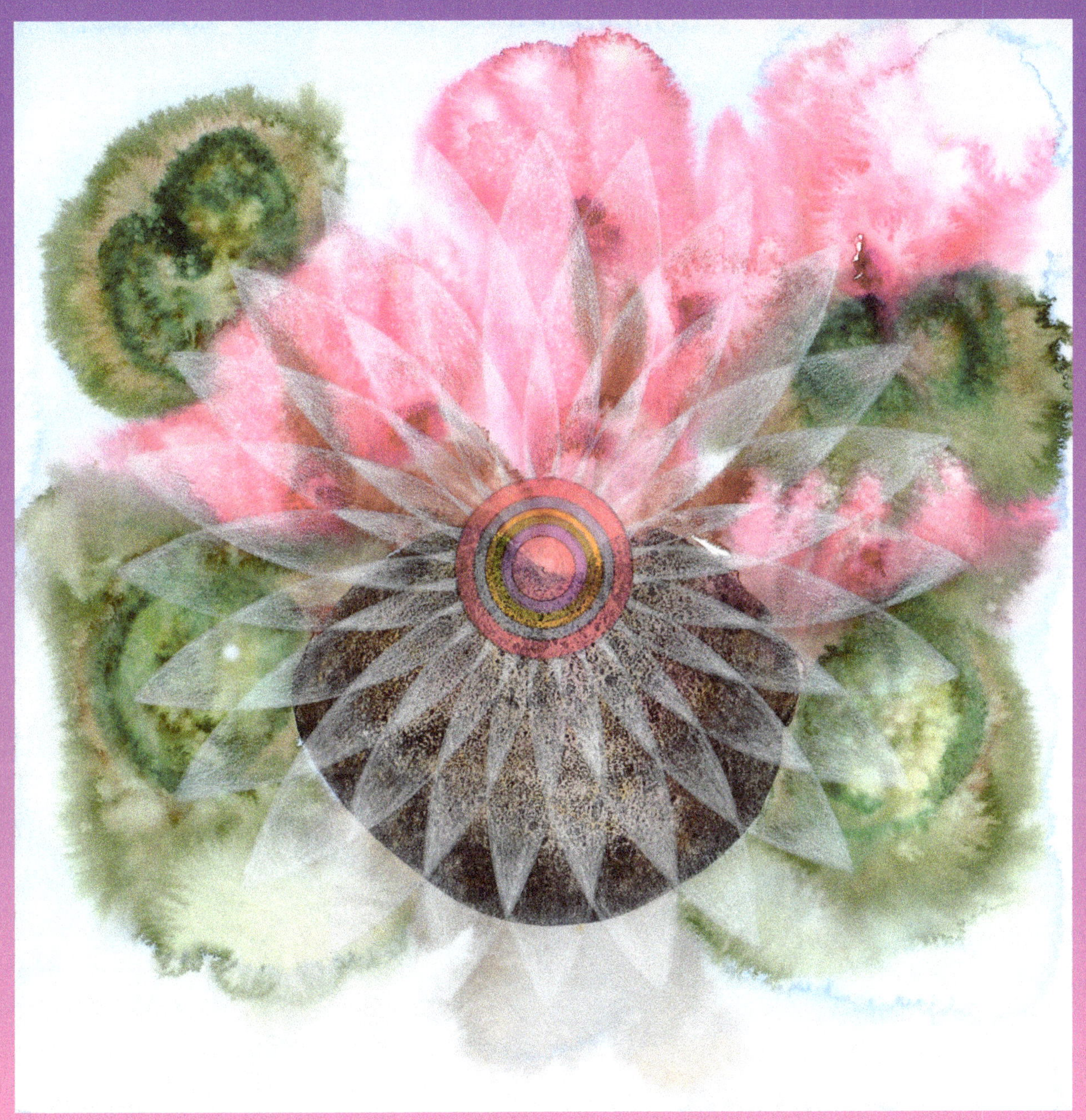

CYCLAMENS COMING OUT OF A BIG HEART

BUDDING

Have you ever gone through a rough time
and wanted to lay your head
on a mothering shoulder
and be told that everything was going to be alright?
These iris buds appeared to me during one of those moments,
bringing me love and care
during a wave of feeling alone.
This was the message which came:
All the iris are here for you
to comfort and care for you.
They are here for you, budding mothers all.
For years I have gotten so excited
whenever I see the buds of flowers.
Perhaps it's the potential they embody.
It's fun to watch
for the flower buds which appear in our own life,
as a reflection of our budding potential ready to bloom.
Just to notice flowers budding,
is a mirror of our own budding.
What excitement, what anticipation!

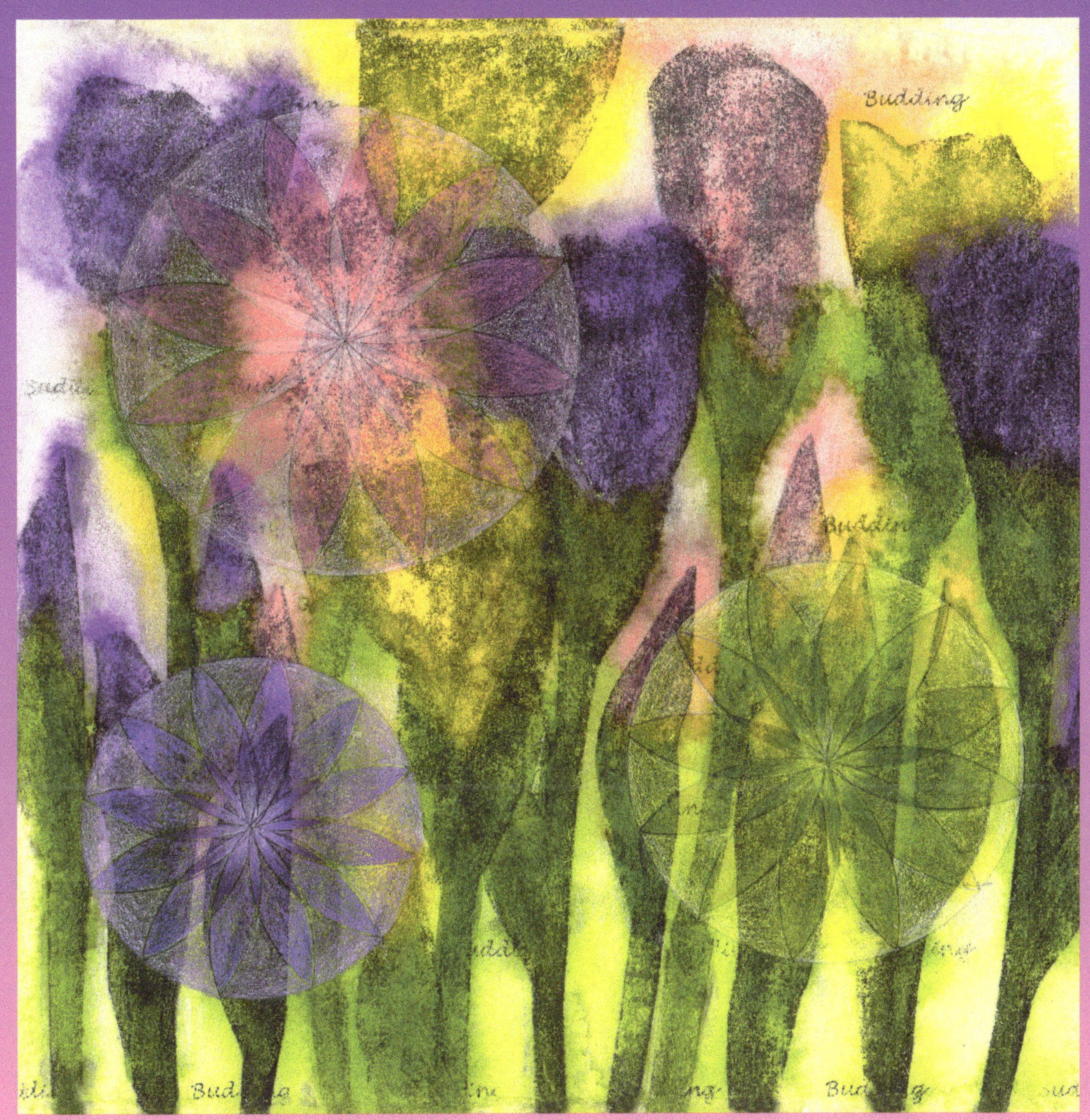

BUDDING

PASSION

When you find your passion,
grab it and throw your arms around it.
Hold it tight and never let it go.
Our passion has a way of getting lost,
amid the trials of every day life.
Sometimes it may be easier
to not light its fire,
especially if we don't know
what to do with the flames.
Passion is a fire that lights up our life,
and allows us to see beauty in all things.
It's why we are alive,
and we need it as our friend.
The flames of passion
must never be doused,
it can break our spirit.
Those flames open doors, open our hearts and
open our eyes wide.
They are our spark, our inner glow.
When we feel passion strongly,
we allow the fire of love
to transport us to a higher realm
which resides in our hearts,
and opens us to ecstasy.

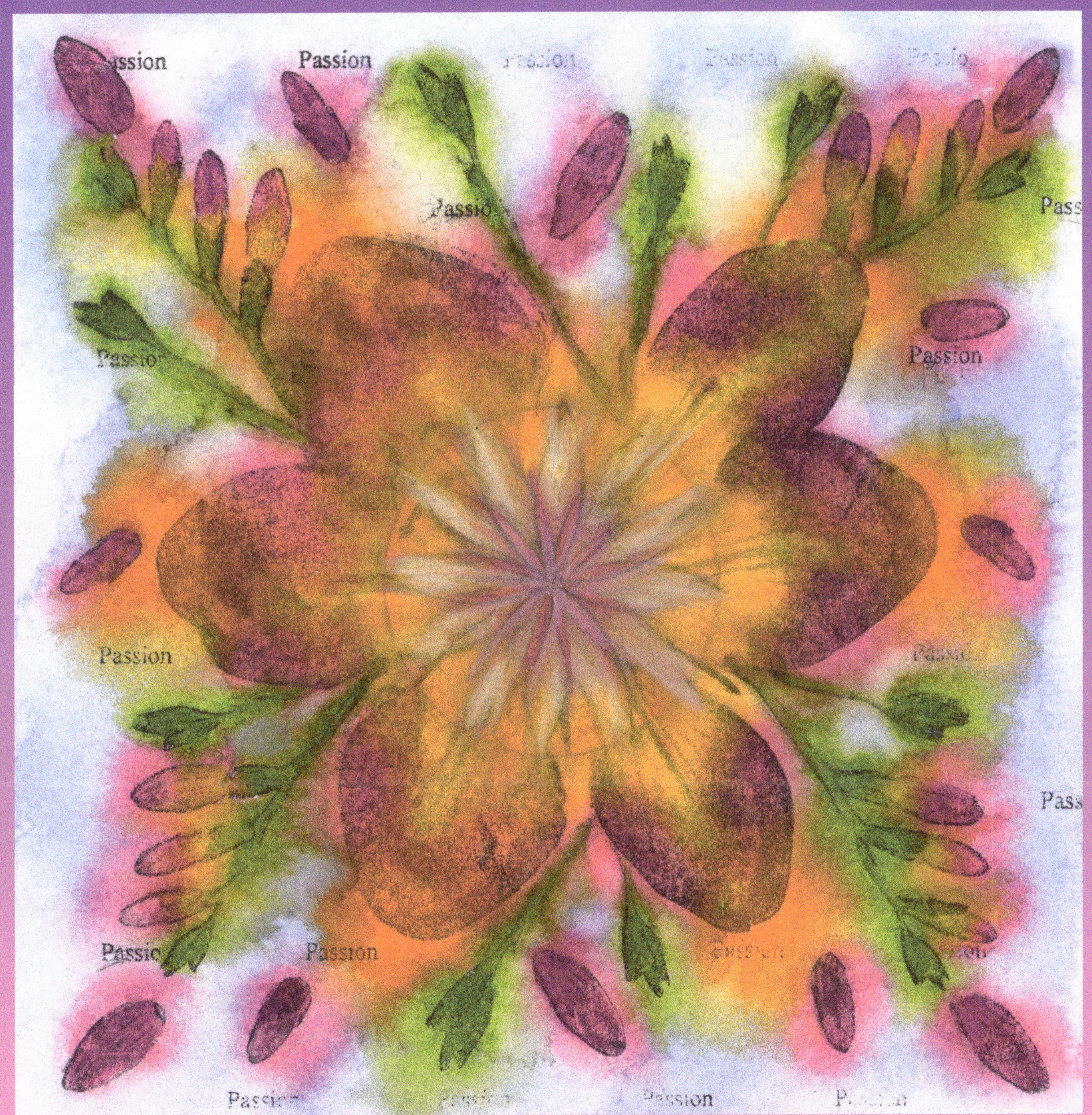

PASSION

THE HEALING OF
THE DARKNESS FLOWER

It's amazing to me that art
can heal our trauma and our old wounds.
It's a process like any other journey,
taking us on hills and valleys,
on rough roads and long highways.
The end result is that a work of art is created,
and it's not really the "end."
It is a culmination of emotions
in the form of colors, songs, dances or stories,
formed from feelings,
all released, alive and breathing
into an art which is alive.
What a release and what freedom
when a new language is born,
with a song from the soul, or a drawing from the heart.
It's a reinterpretation of the memory,
with brighter colors and new words.
Profound and cathartic, this art heals.
Now we can feel our light glow within,
it was always there,
connected to the matrix of Eternal Light.
Here the ancient Flower of Life,
holds us in the sacred Circle of Light.
We are safe, we are loved.
We always have been.
We are Spirit.

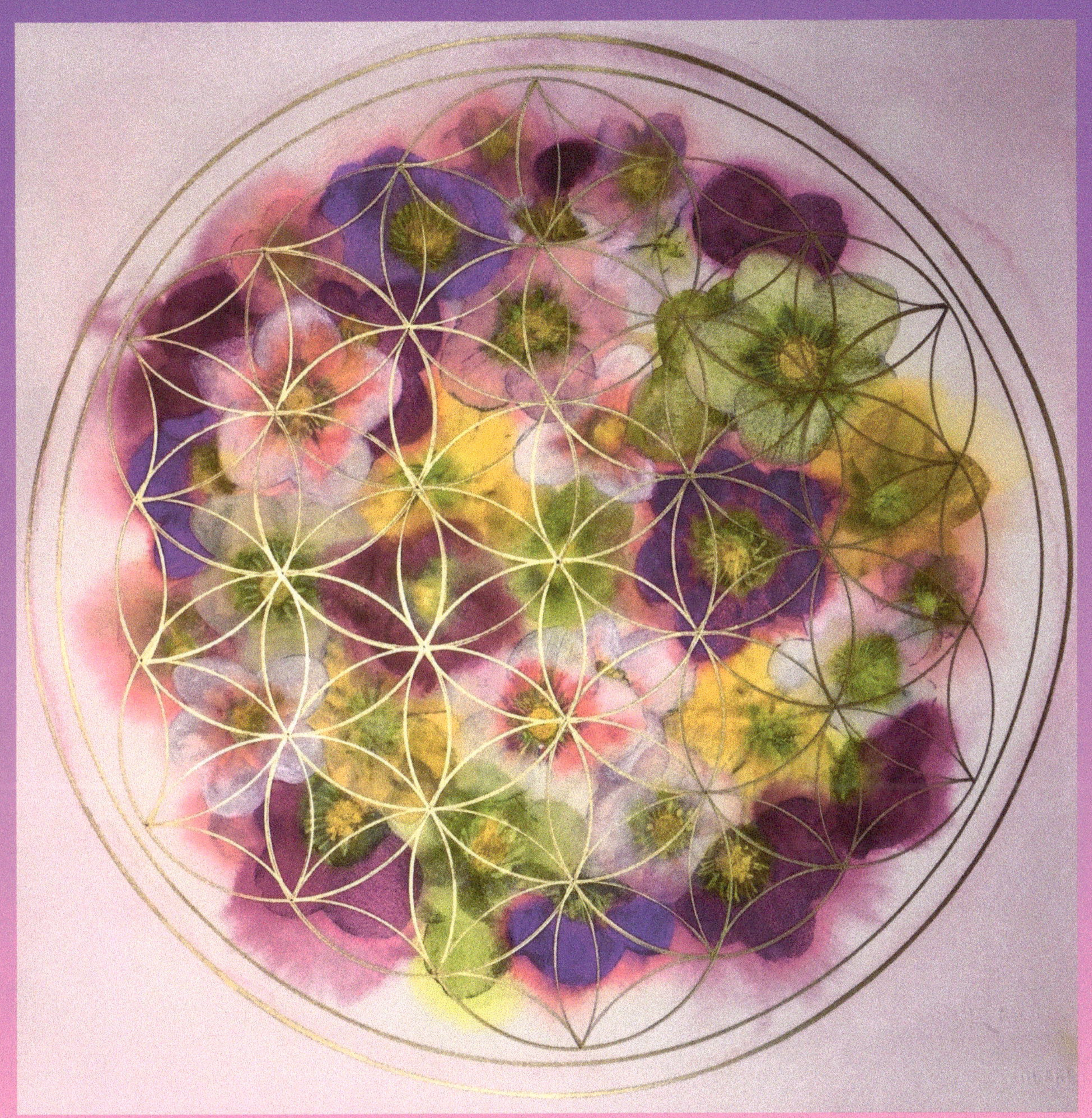

THE HEALING OF THE DARKNESS FLOWER

FEEL IT TO HEAL IT

I believed I could get through life
by not feeling my emotions.
They felt so big and powerful
and, besides,
I thought that feelings were bad.
I learned the hard way
that since I didn't acknowledge my feelings,
I buried them in my body,
and that eventually made me sick.
One day I had a vision
of red tulip buds overlaid
with a geometric pattern.
The first message that came
with those other-worldly flowers was "pain."
Wanting what I considered
a more positive message, I waited.
I saw "feel," or maybe it was "feelings,"
and then realized it was "feel feelings!"
As I completed the painting,
I smiled when the message "feel it to heal it"
came through loud and clear.
Not the easiest thing to do for a stuffer,
but it saved my life.

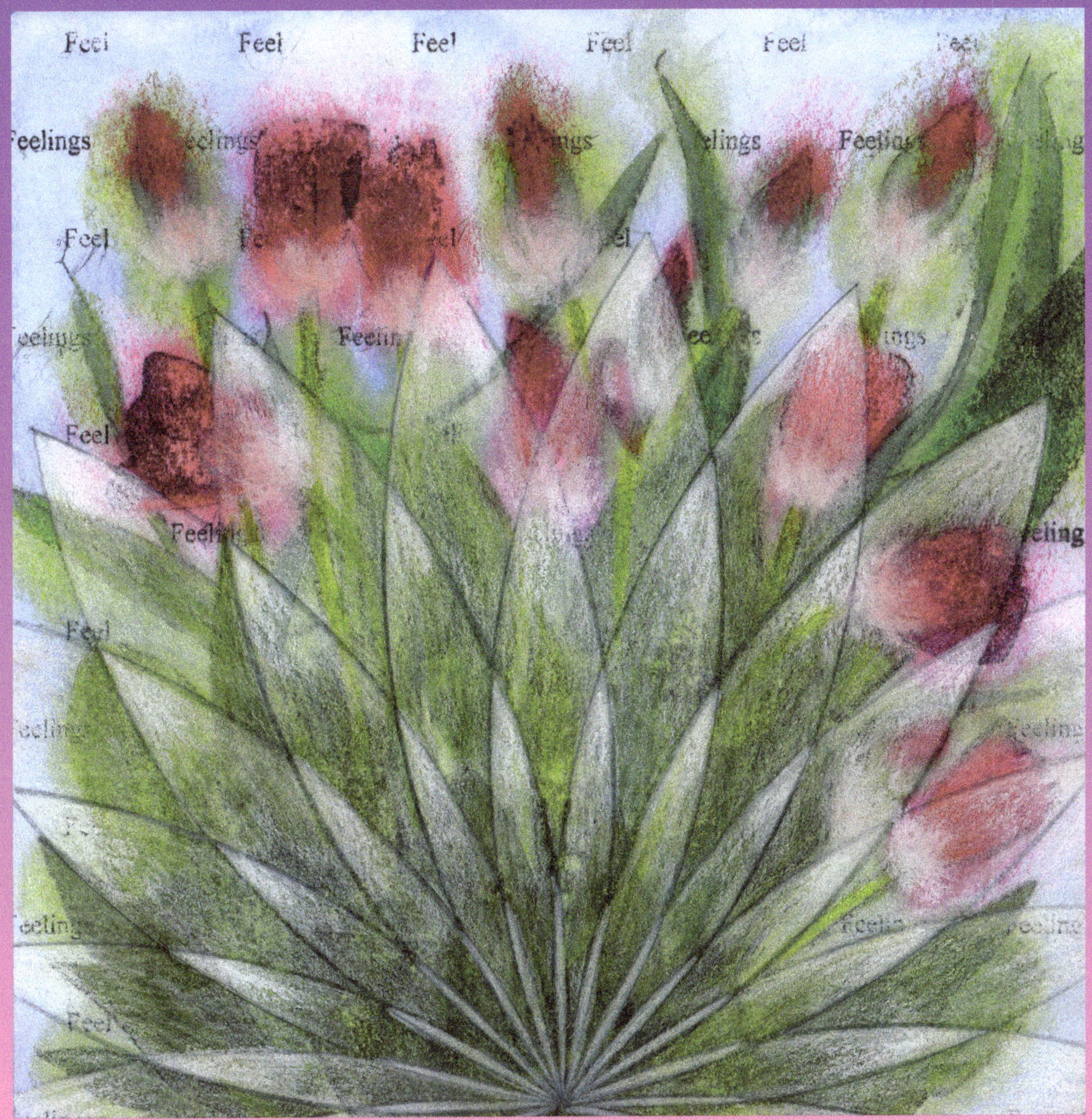

FEEL IT TO HEAL IT

SHOW HER WHAT HELPS

Help came as a beautiful vision of multicolored primroses
with big, bright, smiling yellow centers.
Why did I need help?
The primroses said they were there
to show me how to stop self-criticism.
I am not so plagued anymore
by the shadow which used to sit on my shoulder
ready to pounce at any perceived wavering outside the lines.
Thinking she was helping me,
my little scared one inside
was diligent, having learned criticism
from those she thought were in-the-know.
But those weren't in-the-know and just repeated
their ancestors' less-than-positive patterns.
"It doesn't have to be that way anymore,"
my grandma would tell me in dreams,
and she kept up the visitations until I got it.
Beautifully vivid, precious and full of love,
being touched by primroses changes and alters.
I now jump in and swim in the pool of rippling color when I need help.
I remember the vision of bright flowers with smiling yellow centers
and bathe myself with the colors
which uplift my spirit and take the gray away.
Primroses always offer a wash of bright color and healing.
They delight me and make me smile.
I accept their gift!

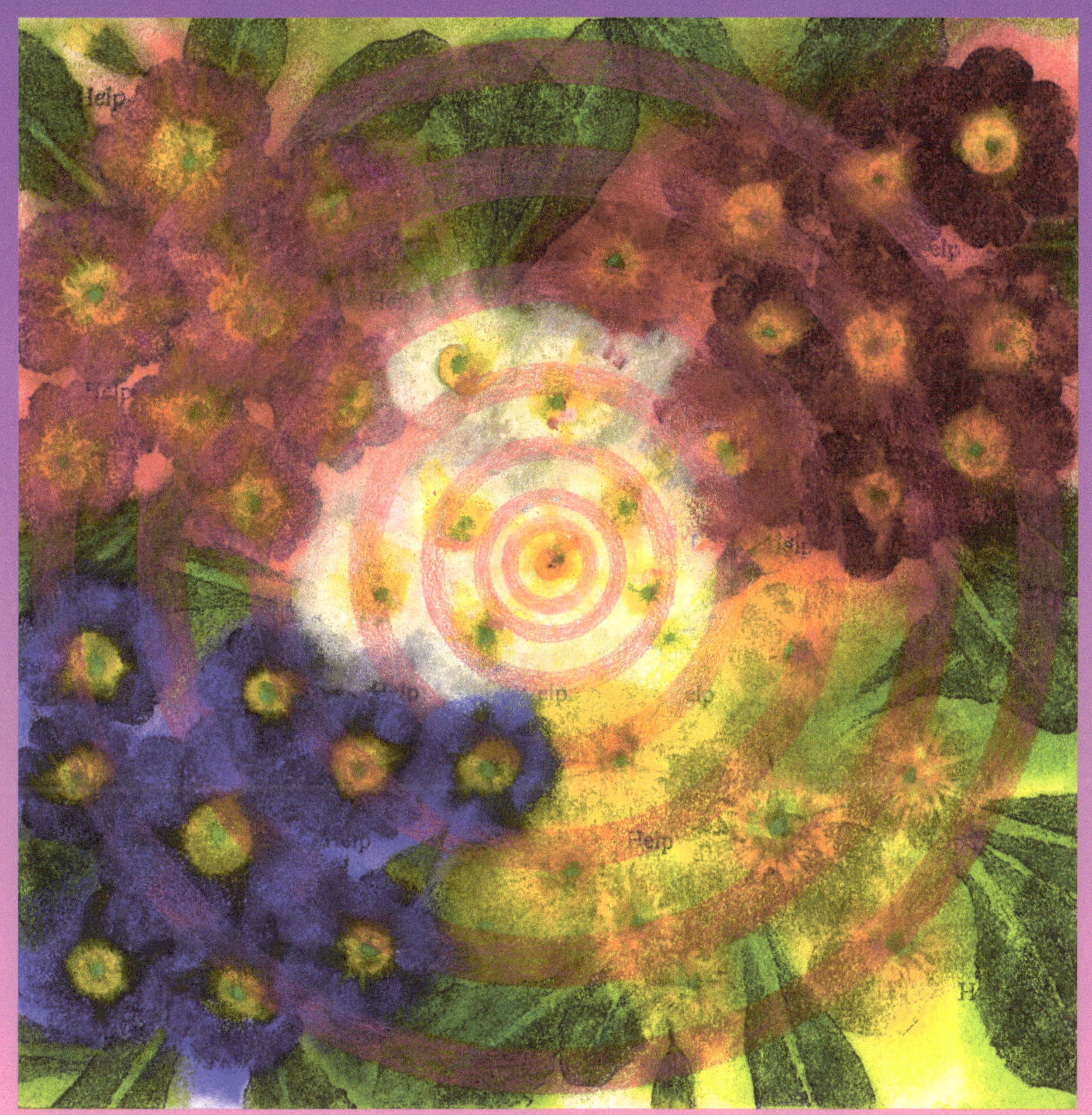

SHOW HER WHAT HELPS

THERE IS A HEALING GOING ON

Can we learn
from the ephemeral dandelion
to let go?
To relax and allow healing?
To allow Spirit
to flow *through* our bodies
in a dynamic and yet effortless way?
These wispy dandelions
bring us an ethereal gift.
Can we let go to it?
Overlaid with the
the Genesis pattern of the Flower of Life,
they represent
the genesis of infinite creativity
and infinite healing.

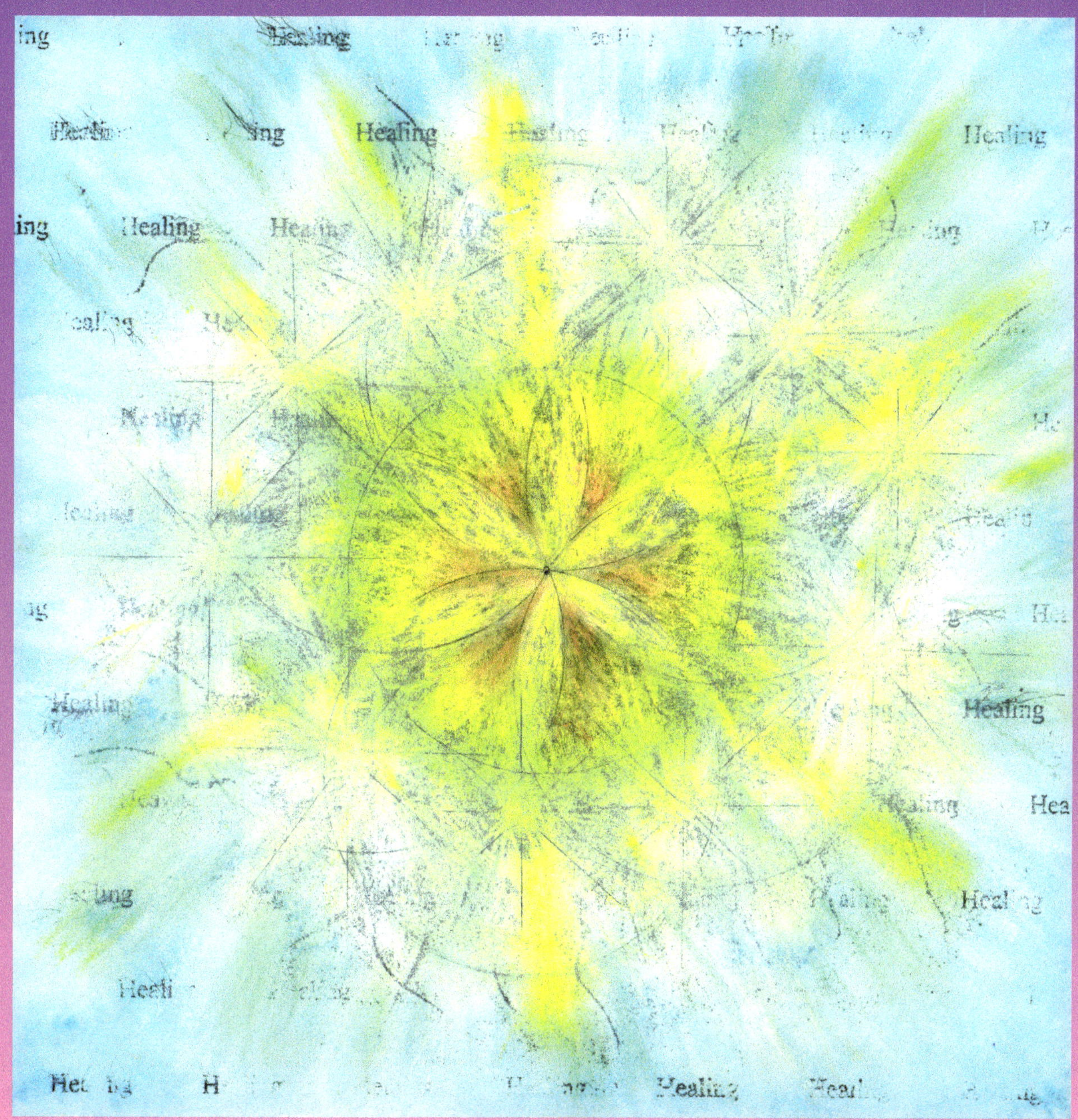

THERE IS A HEALING GOING ON

THOUGHTS ARE THINGS

In my mind's eye,
I saw a pansy one day,
in the midst of some
dark fear thoughts.
I asked it,
"Have you a message for me?"
It replied,
Thoughts are things
they have wings
let them fly away.
Let the love in.
Look at the pansy
and tell me that isn't a loving face
smiling love on you.
Let it in.
And be joyous for that gift.
After that beautiful message, I really enjoyed painting the pansies.
Can you see them, there are more than one?
I love pansies.
They are a favorite of my mother's.

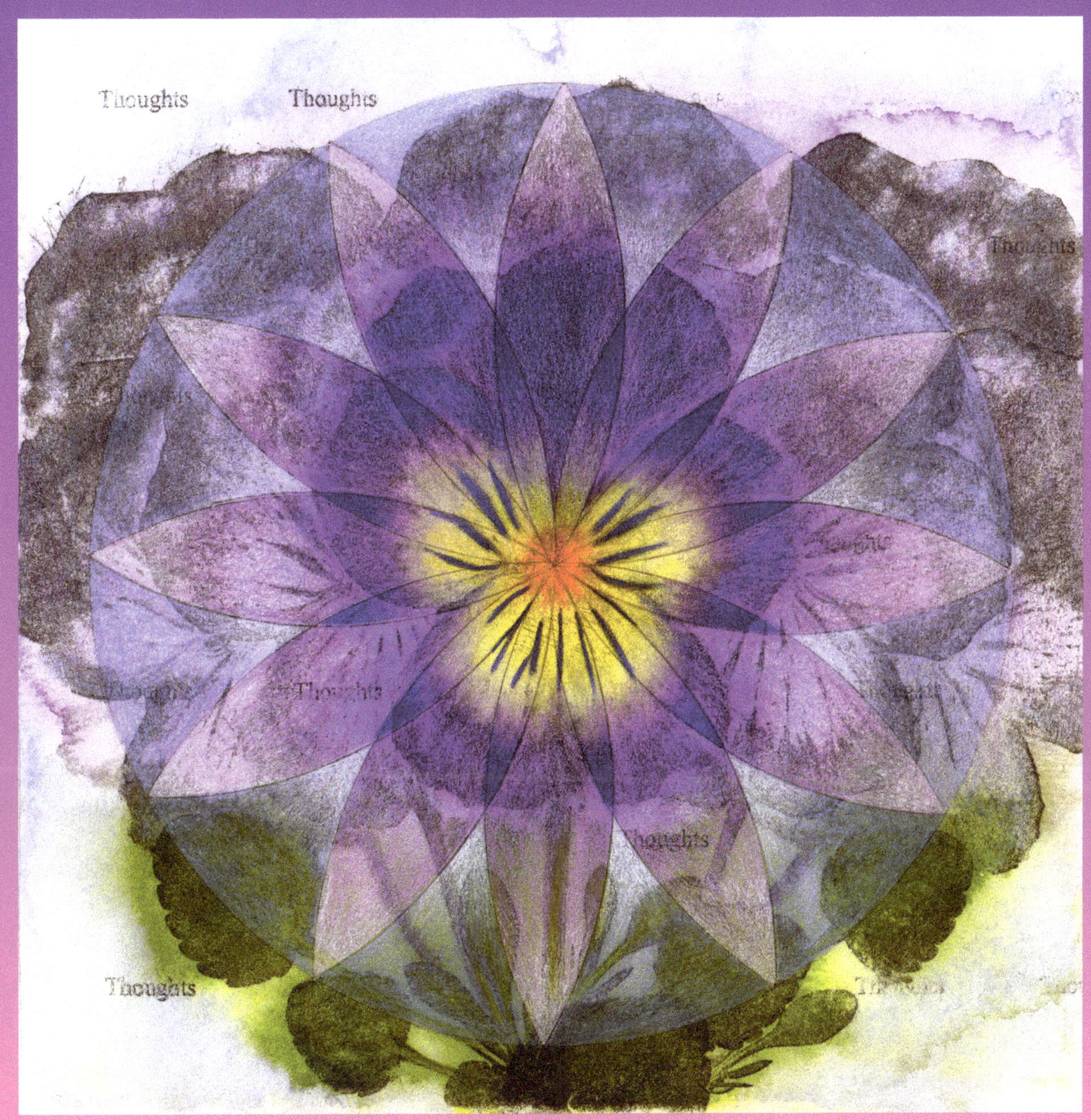

THOUGHTS ARE THINGS

NURTURE ME WHERE I LIVE

The Midnight Tears Orchid
rests beautifully in the creative cavity
of the pelvic bone where life begins.
At the center, the tear is like a droplet of light
which ignites creation.
This flower spoke to me deeply with its midnight tears,
it was acknowledging, comforting and soothing.
In my youth I wish I'd had more of my creative spark nurtured,
and I shed a lot of tears because it wasn't.
In the shape of a seed, the tear, the droplet of light,
holds so much energy and love.
It's alive with creative potential.
Where does the spark of our own seed come from?
It's there and all it needs to grow is nurturing.
Representing infinite creativity,
the ancient Seed of Life symbol shows us
the connection we all have to the Divine matrix.
We are all one, all connected,
all a unique pattern within ourselves,
but all part of the One, and all infinitely creative.
I understand now the importance of nurturing
the spark of creativity which feeds and nurtures.
I see it in the depths of the orchid and its tear.
My seed was fed, nurtured and strengthened by my tears.
Creativity abounds when it is nurtured.
With freedom to create, I soar.

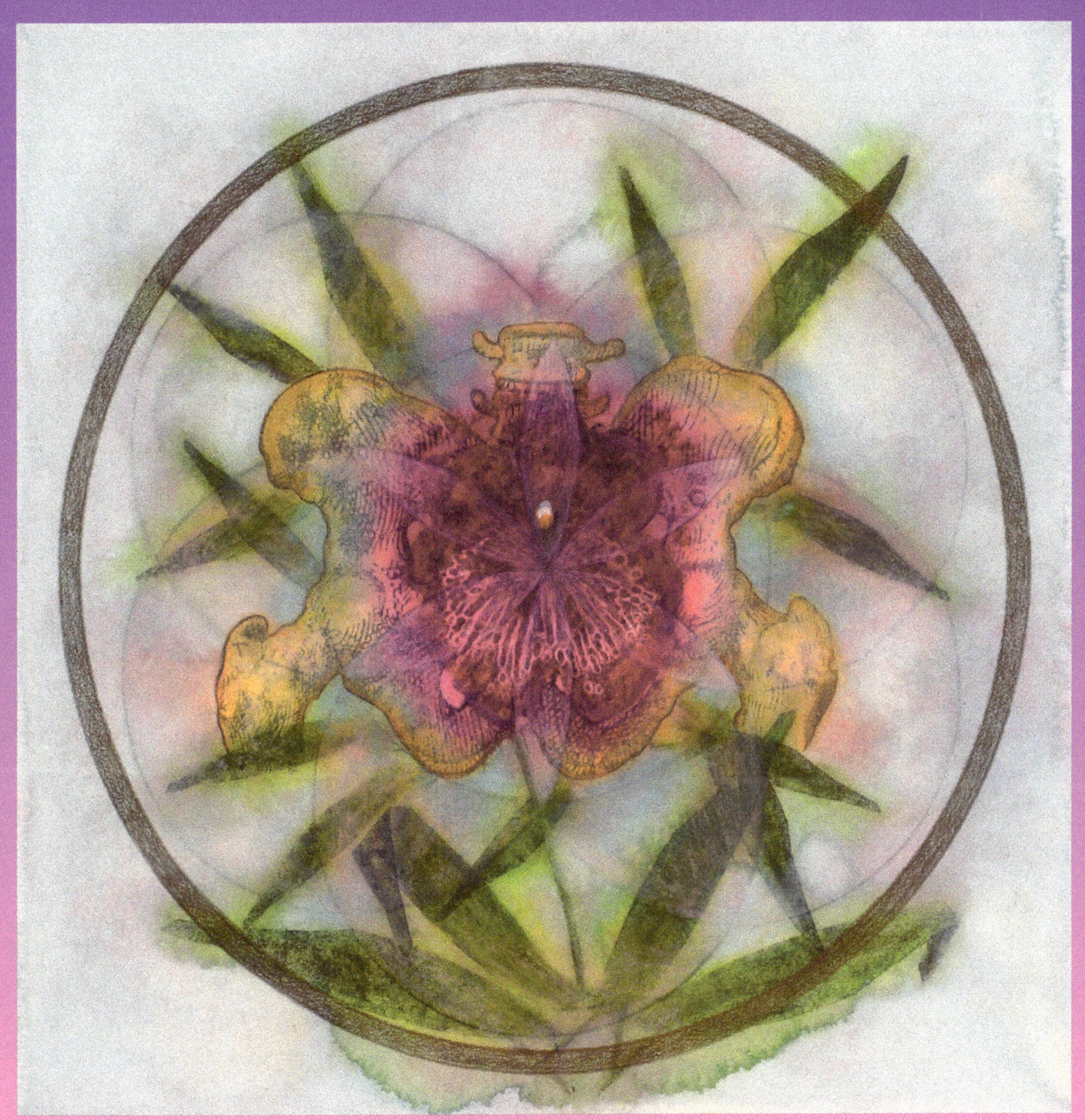

NURTURE ME WHERE I LIVE AND LET ME FLY

RELEASE

In the middle of the night
I was awakened by a headache.
It was at the back of my head. and it held on.
It's not unusual for me to hold tension there
but it did get my attention.
What *was* unusual were the calla lilies I saw,
in various colors,
dancing and cupped around
the back of my skull and neck.
I relaxed with the coming of the lilies,
and their stunning magnificence.
Beautiful, colorful butterflies were then
released from my head.
They floated away and the tension lifted.
What a sight, what a night, and what relief!
You could not see my smile in the dark,
but it was there.

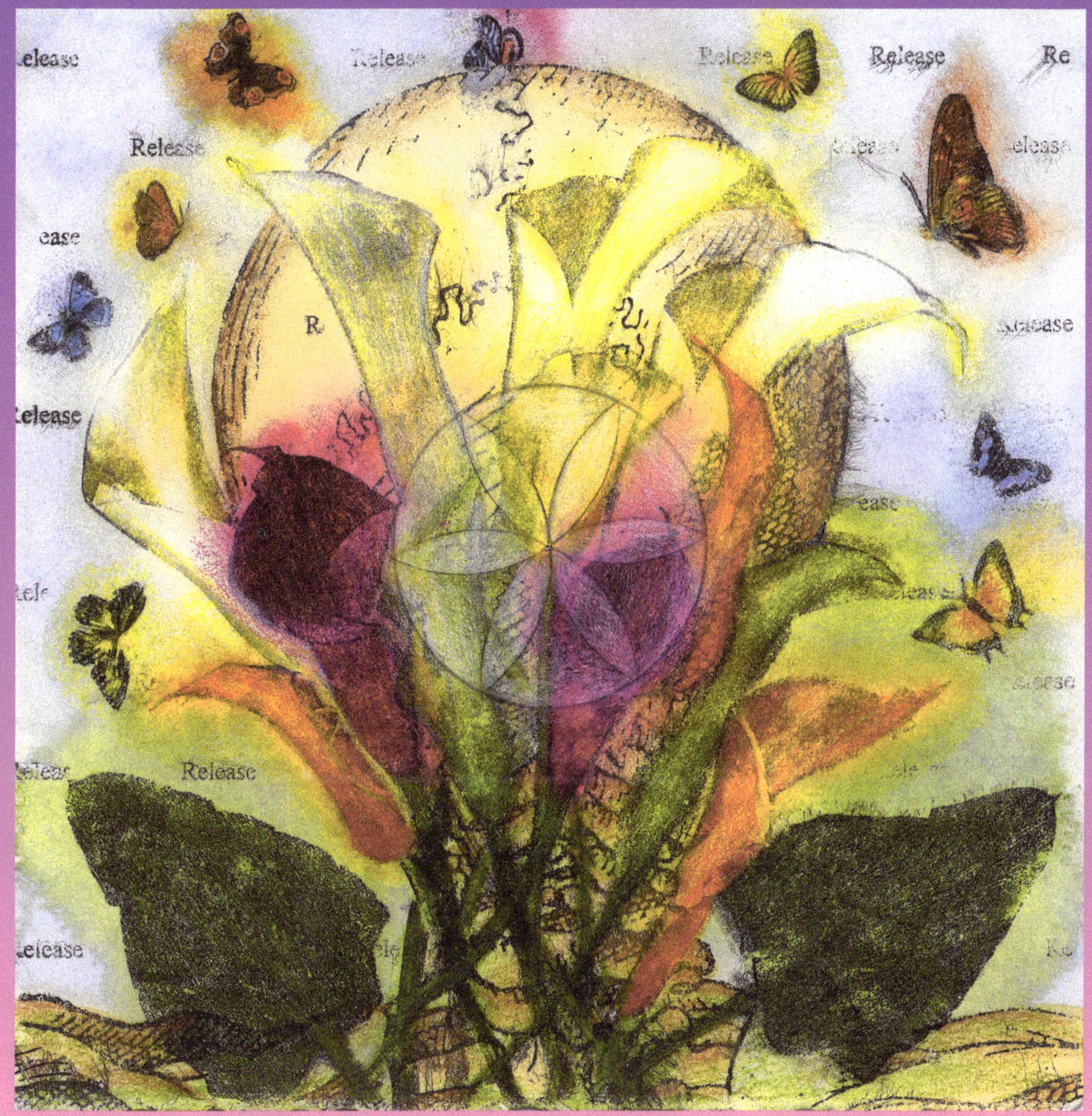

RELEASE

THE FLOWERING
OF ENCOURAGEMENT

It's a flurry of flowers.
Hydrangeas are sprinkling good dust.
The floating petals and leaves
offer encouragement with
such beautiful softness and care.
There is courage in encouragement,
hailing from the word *cœur*,
heart and spirit.
These hydrangeas dreamily cast their gifts
of Divine blossoms.
They touch the Sacred Heart,
and not just the one, but everyone's heart.
All are sacred.
I love scattering flowers,
as far back as a flower girl in my aunts' weddings,
but then more focused on the mess,
than the offering.
Not only do I love tossing flowers,
I love spreading encouragement.
Tending to give it over-abundantly,
I suppose I am making up for lost opportunities.
Now I hold the basket of petals courageously,
and with beauty of intent and the good dust,
I welcome every opportunity to spread love, blessings
and encouragement of heart and spirit,
far and wide.

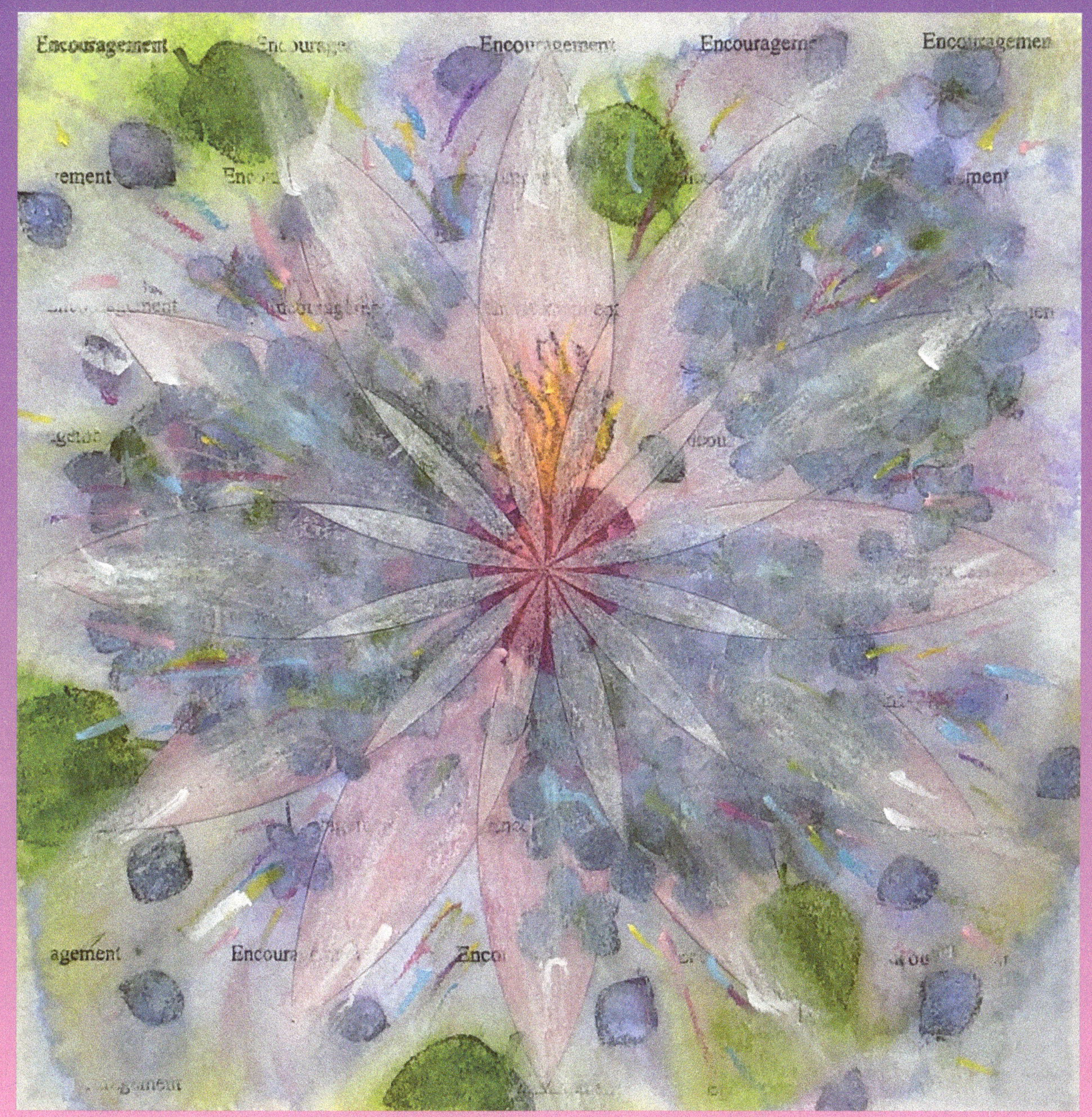

THE FLOWERING OF ENCOURAGEMENT

AMARYLLIS, ANEMONE, LETTUCE
AND THE NEED FOR STARS

The spiritual sustenance and light
available to us from flowers and vegetables
is miraculous and rich.
This amaryllis bud is a symbol of that light.
She is like a kind inner mother,
a pillar of light and strength,
who teaches us to be kind to ourselves
and provides us with
the best nutrients for our growth.
Anemone flowers and lettuce,
in the garden of life,
are also fed by the light of the stars.
Witness the star petunias overhead.
Let us remember to look up,
and receive with amazement and gratitude,
the stardust and the light that fills
every living thing on earth.
It's the best nutrition!

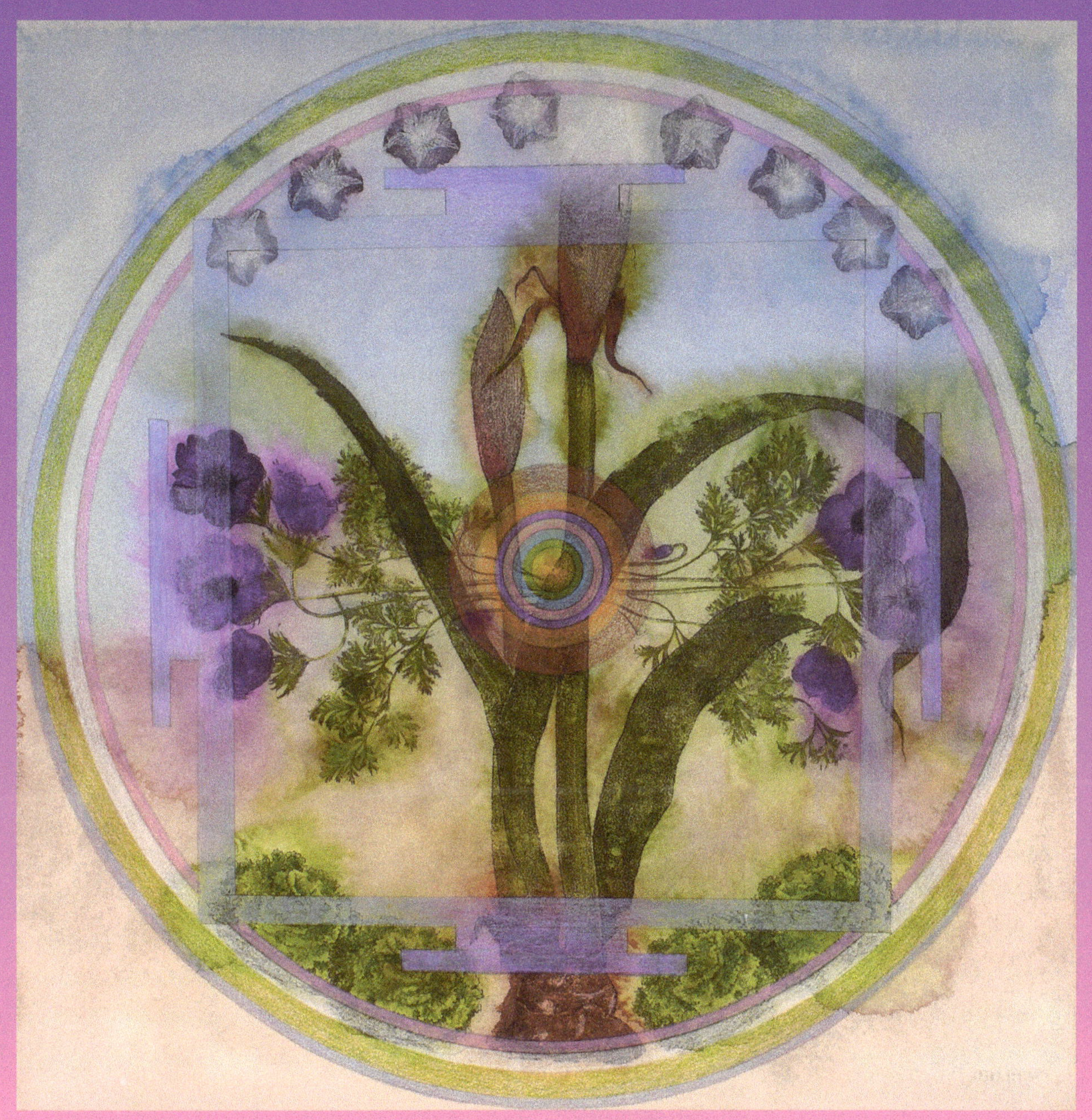

AMARYLLIS, ANEMONE, LETTUCE AND THE NEED FOR STARS

REACHING FOR THE LIGHT

These yellow calla lilies are reaching for the light–
opening up to bloom to their fullest.
Come out and be who you are;
come out and play,
was their message to me.
Sometimes we may want
to remain turned inward
like the yet unbloomed flower.
You can come out now!
the calla lilies say.
Like these beautiful yellow flowers,
it's time to reach for the light,
open, play and
show our beauty.

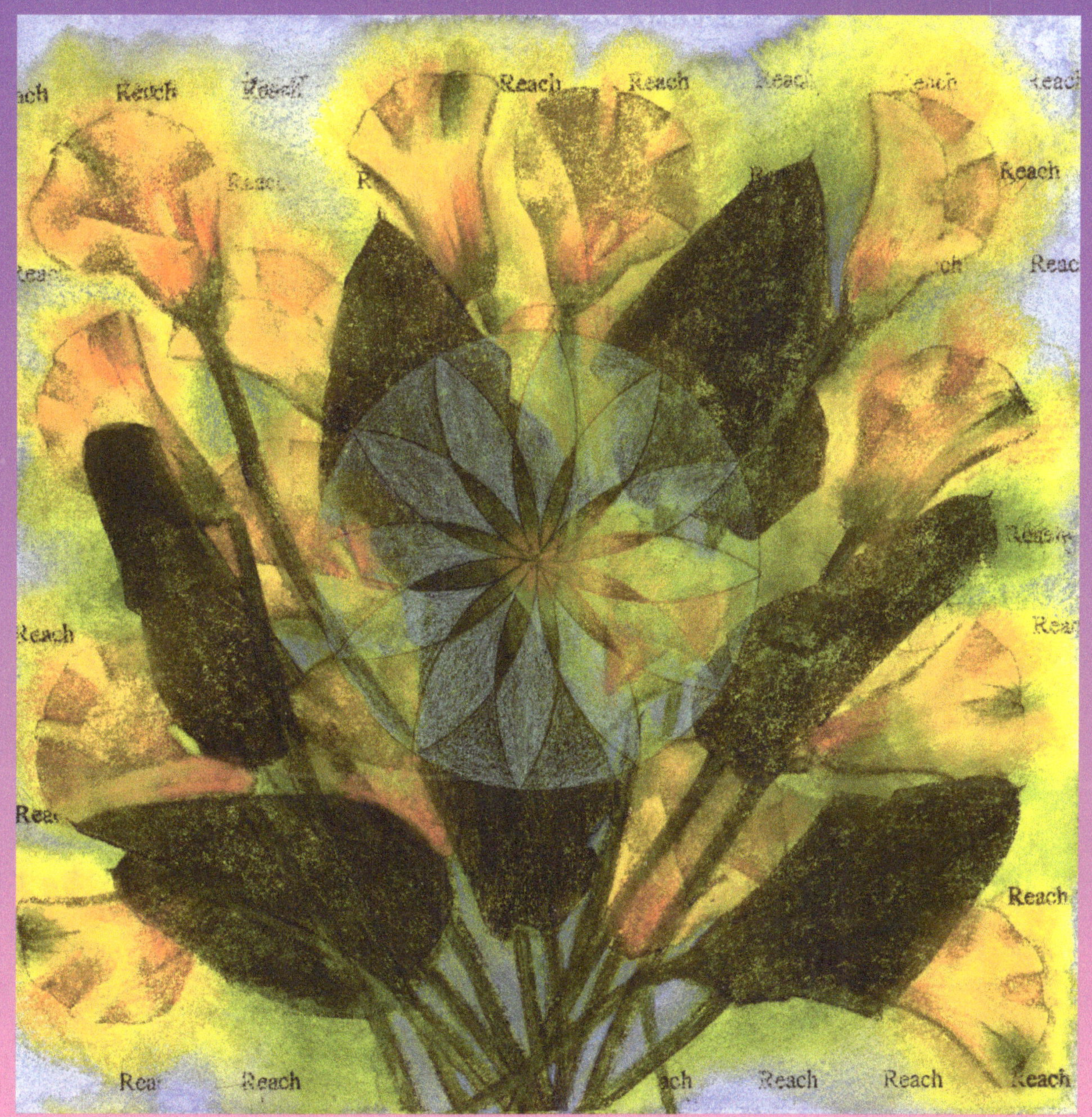

REACHING FOR THE LIGHT

THE OFFERING

My intention was to co-create
a mandala of Peace and Healing
from the vision I saw of
rose leaves, olive leaves and lime.
It seemed to be an offering.
The elements came from my garden,
and over the painting I drew a center circle,
divided it into five equals,
and added five more circles.
Why did I do that?
I don't know, I can't say for sure.
That's the mystery of mandalas,
especially when co-created with Spirit.
This one gave me an unexpected star in the center.
What a gift, and I was pleased.
The circles created a kind of aura,
a magic bubble,
a prism of light to see the mandala through.
It was comforting and peaceful,
both to create, and to witness.
What was its message?
For me it was to be grateful
for what I am offered.
Even if, at first, it seems like a mystery.

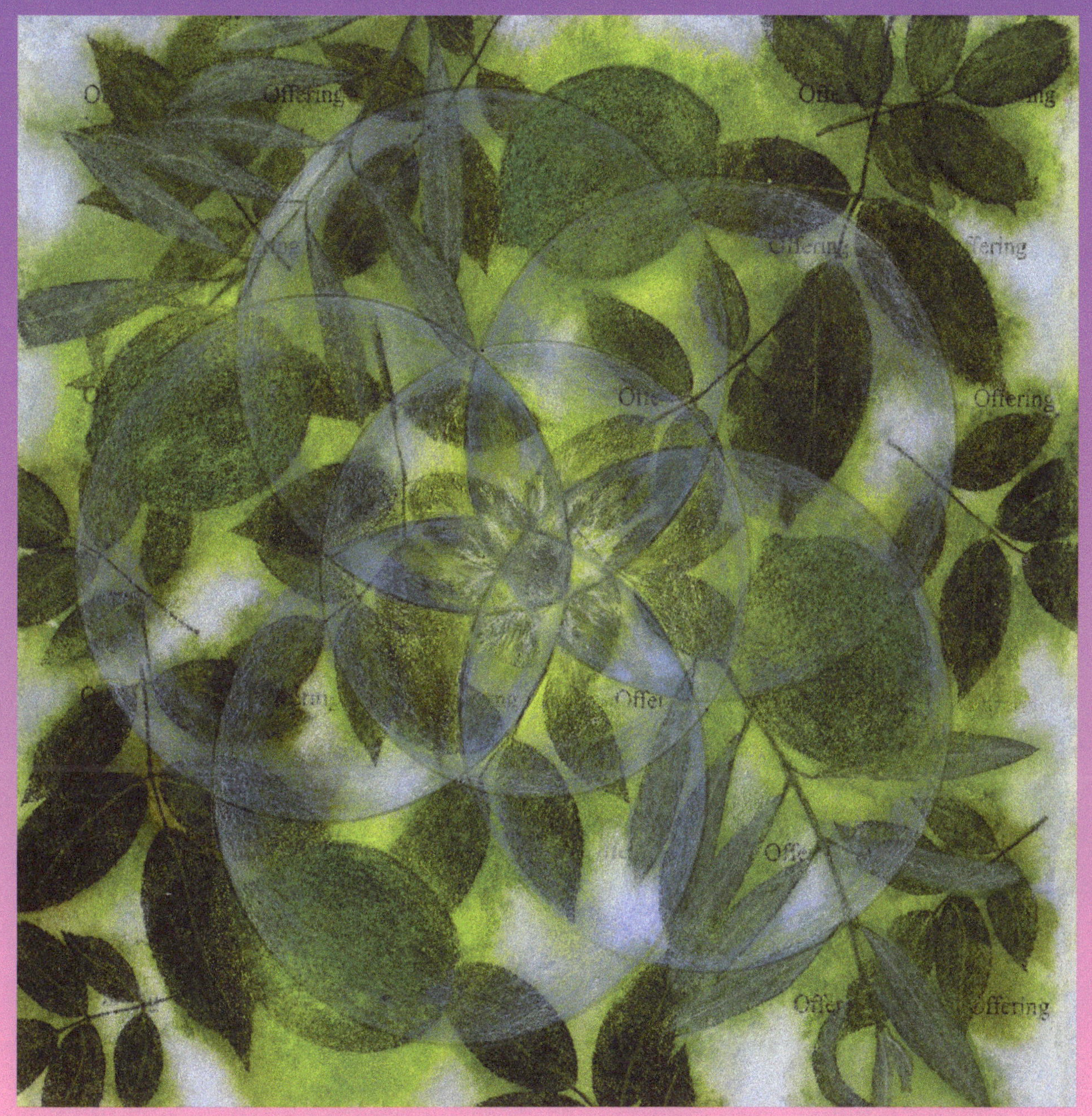

THE OFFERING: OLIVE BRANCHES, LIMELIGHT AND THE STAR

EXPANDING MY KALEIDOSCOPE VISION

This kaleidoscope vision surprised me.
It wasn't what I expected or assigned!
In class, while encouraging everyone to follow their own guidance,
I would usually offer an example of how I approached the assignment.
This time was no different.
The week's lesson was the second chakra,
the orange, flower-like spinning energy at our creative center.
I was anxious to paint what I had seen.
The moving, charged image which had appeared to me in such a wild flash.
I wanted to be bold and use violets with the orange,
but how was I going to avoid making mud when these opposites
would inevitably encounter each other on my wet paper?
I soaked it in the bathtub, my drawing done with glitter pen,
and painted over the top of it soaking wet.
Was I courageous or just plain crazy?
It moved, it expanded, it mixed, it exploded and it worked!
There is only one way to paint a moving kaleidoscope,
and it's from our own vision, ours alone.
When looking through a kaleidoscope,
the minutest shift in focus, will change the image,
and it becomes a new view. Nothing remains the same.
Each pattern is as compelling and as beautiful as the next.
Change is the constant, and there is always another perspective.
It's a beautiful metaphor.
With just a thought, a breath, a slight twist,
our vision can expand.

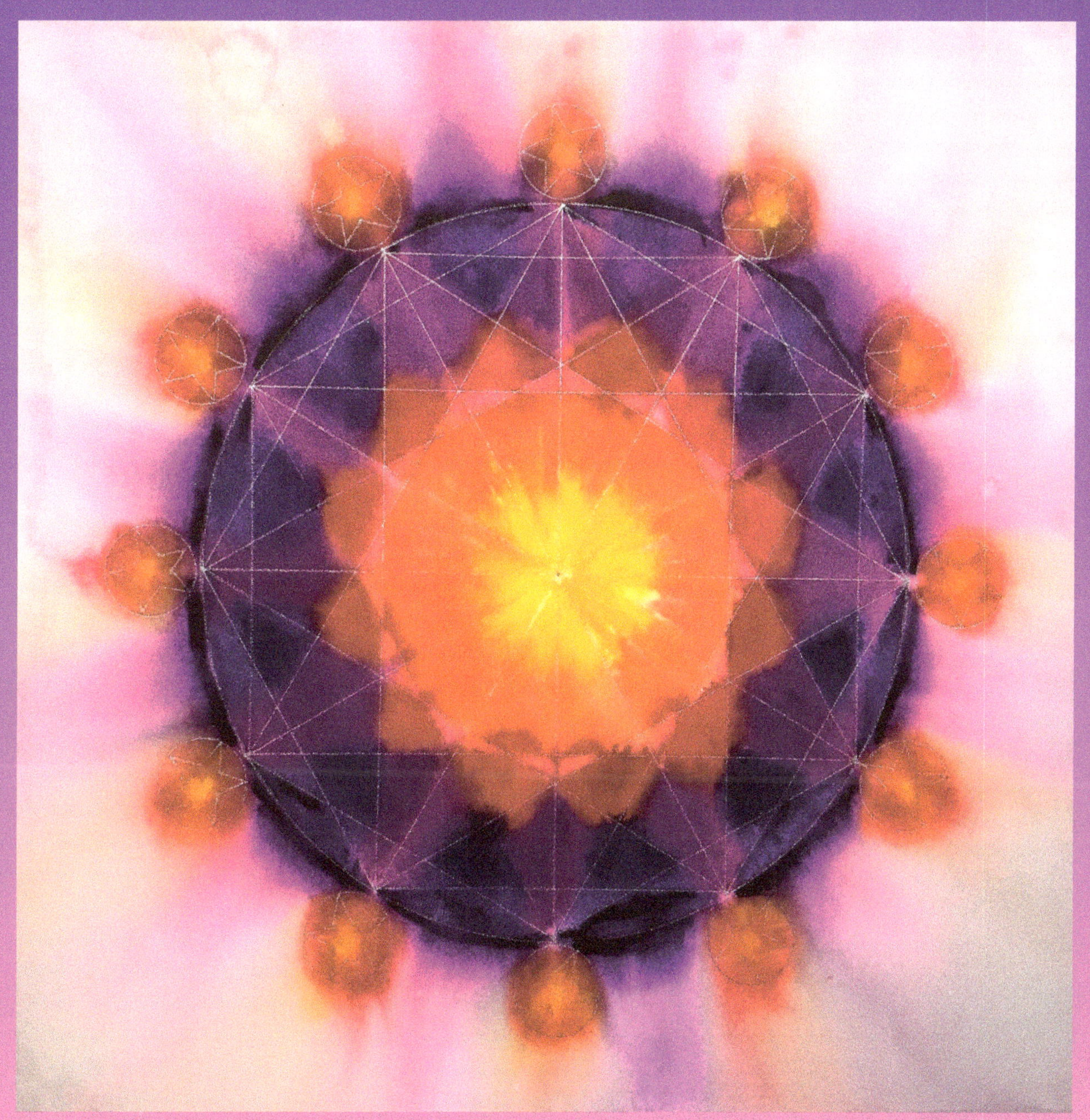

EXPANDING MY KALEIDOSCOPE VISION

BEAUTIFUL, SWEET AND MYSTERIOUS

After receiving numerous visions of orchids,
I wondered why, and asked,
"What are the orchids for?"
These are the words that came:
Healing. Sweetness. Intricate. Mysterious.
Old, ancient, deep knowledge.
I imagined the orchids
growing in, and emerging from, a jungle.
They must have existed for so long,
and seen so much.
And then, out of the depths of the jungle
came such beauty.
Aren't our lives sometimes like a jungle?
I believe I was being told
that we all have the potential to emerge
Beautiful, Sweet and Mysterious.

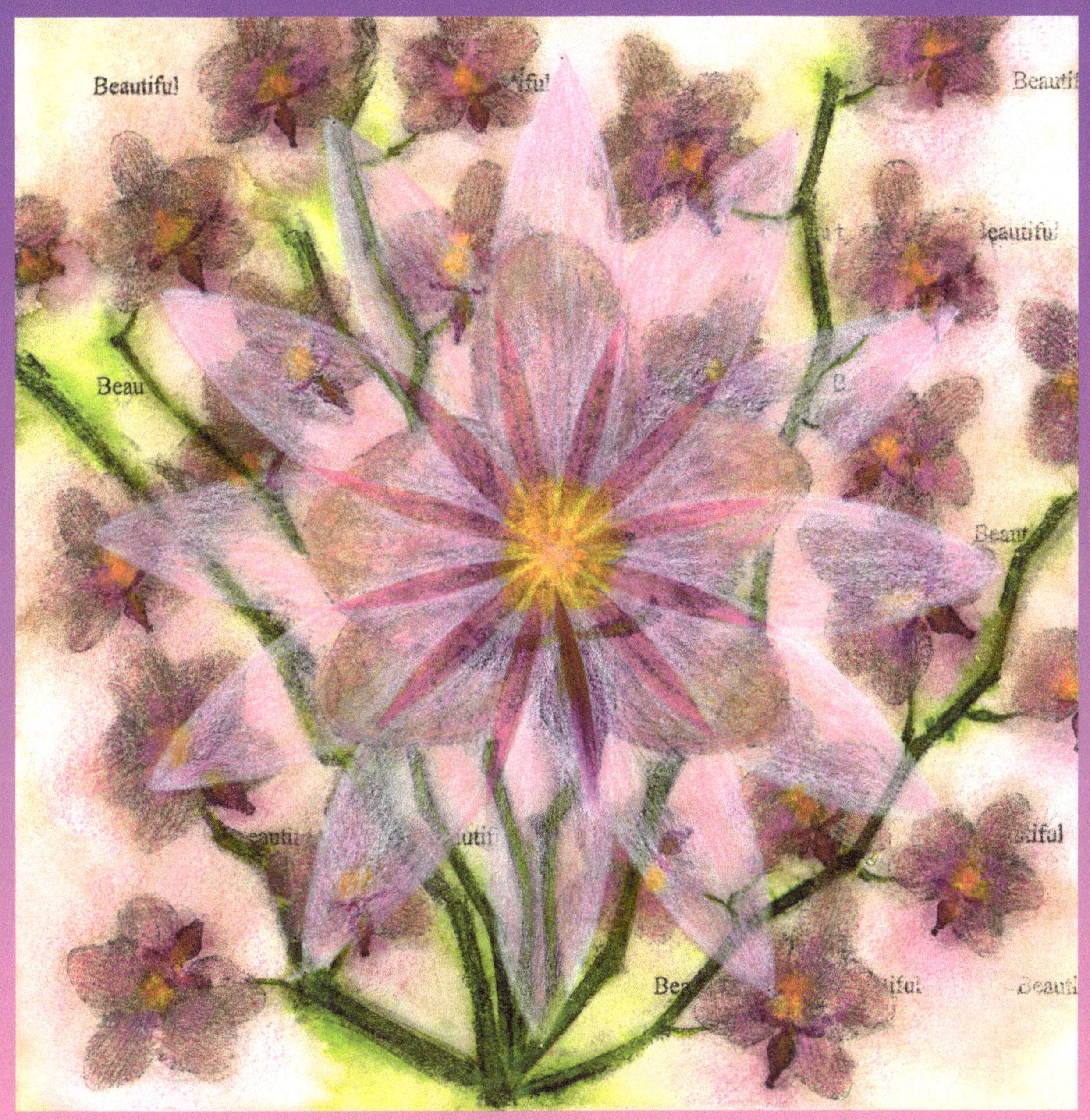

BEAUTIFUL, SWEET AND MYSTERIOUS

MY EGG OF LIFE

This mandala is a Sacred Geometry symbol
of an Egg of Life.
It has 8 circles, but one you can't see
because it's around on the back side.
It represents the 8 cells in our original egg,
which is said to contain our physical characteristics.
I created this mandala as an example
of an exercise which could be used in my classes.
The intention for the mandala in class
was to focus on the parts of ourselves we liked.
What were the things about myself I liked?
It was interesting to contemplate,
and fun to see how it turned out.
Each circle represents something I liked about myself.
If I were to connect the center of all the circles with a line,
it would create a cube.
In Sacred Geometry all life forms
are created out of geometric patterns.
It is a language of truth, beauty, harmony,
proportion, rhythm and order.
This geometry is an ancient science
where everything is in relationship to everything else,
and therefore in relationship to the Divine.

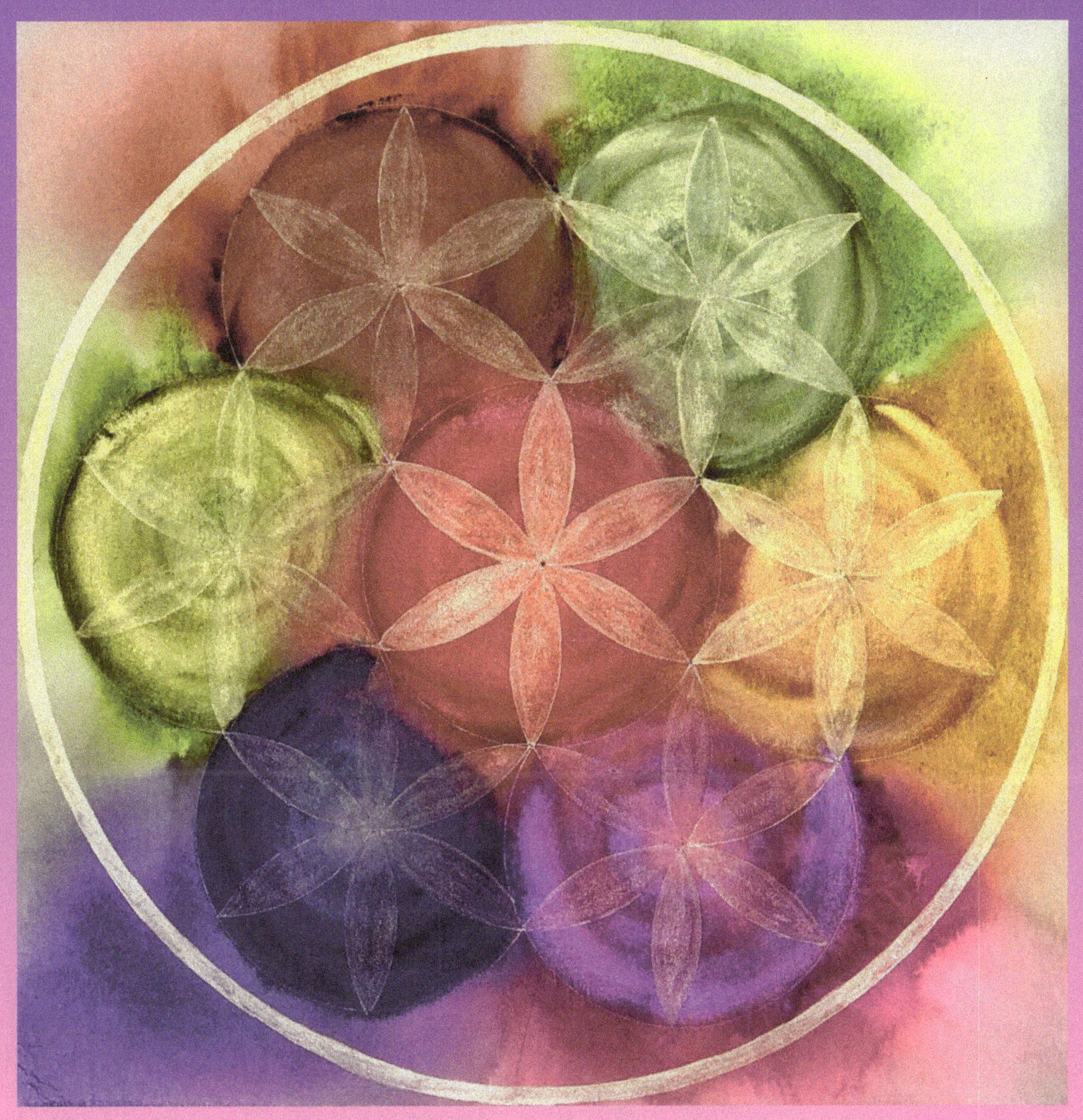

MY EGG OF LIFE

FREE

Freedom.
It's my favorite word.
It has been for longer than I can remember.
This lotus celebrates the freedom to bloom,
rising up from the water to touch the sun.
What liberation, lifting our heads above water!
The lotus to me is a symbol of a Sacred state,
of blooming to our full potential.
It is one of the most awe-inspiring flowers
that has ever been.
Rising up out of the mud toward the sunshine,
a lotus is nourished by the mud,
but not held down by it.
The lotus is the ideal flower
to represent our inner Spirit.
Sacred, resilient and beautiful,
they have always carried an air of mystery,
and have been a symbol of re-birth for centuries.
Nightly they submerge their blossom
into murky water,
and each morning re-bloom without residue,
pure, perfect and free.
A flower for all seasons, all times, all souls,
and me!

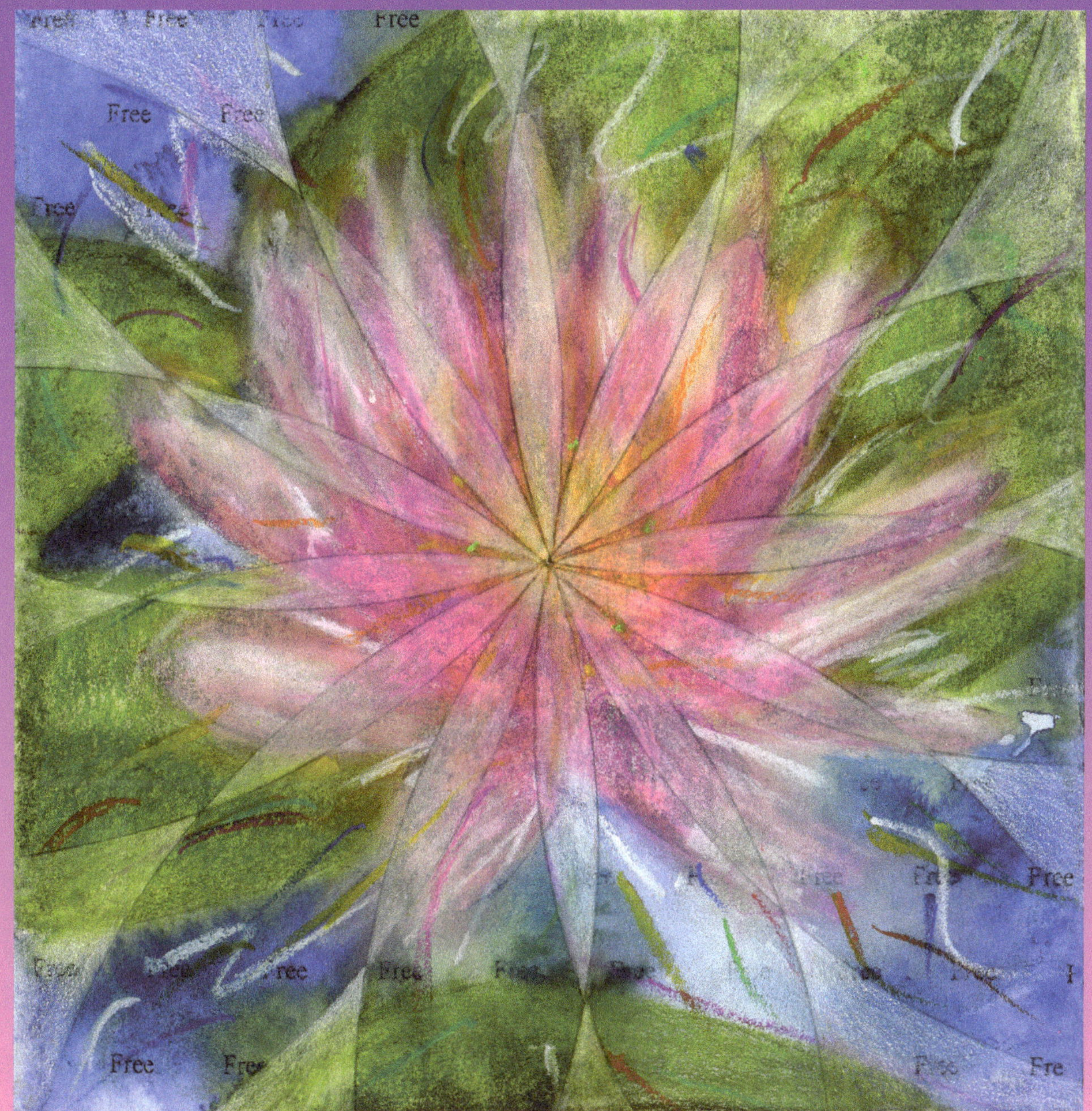

FREE

PEACE

I asked for a spiritual symbol
one New Year's Eve,
as a message for the New Year.
This flower came in a dream that night.
The flower,
a spathiphyllum blossom,
is also called a "peace lily,"
and in this mandala,
is overlaid with a pattern
which is very blossom-like.
The symbol is called a Torus,
and is generated from the movement of a spiraling circle.
Peace.
Peace spiraling outwards,
with a beautiful message,
and a beautiful energy.
Any year.

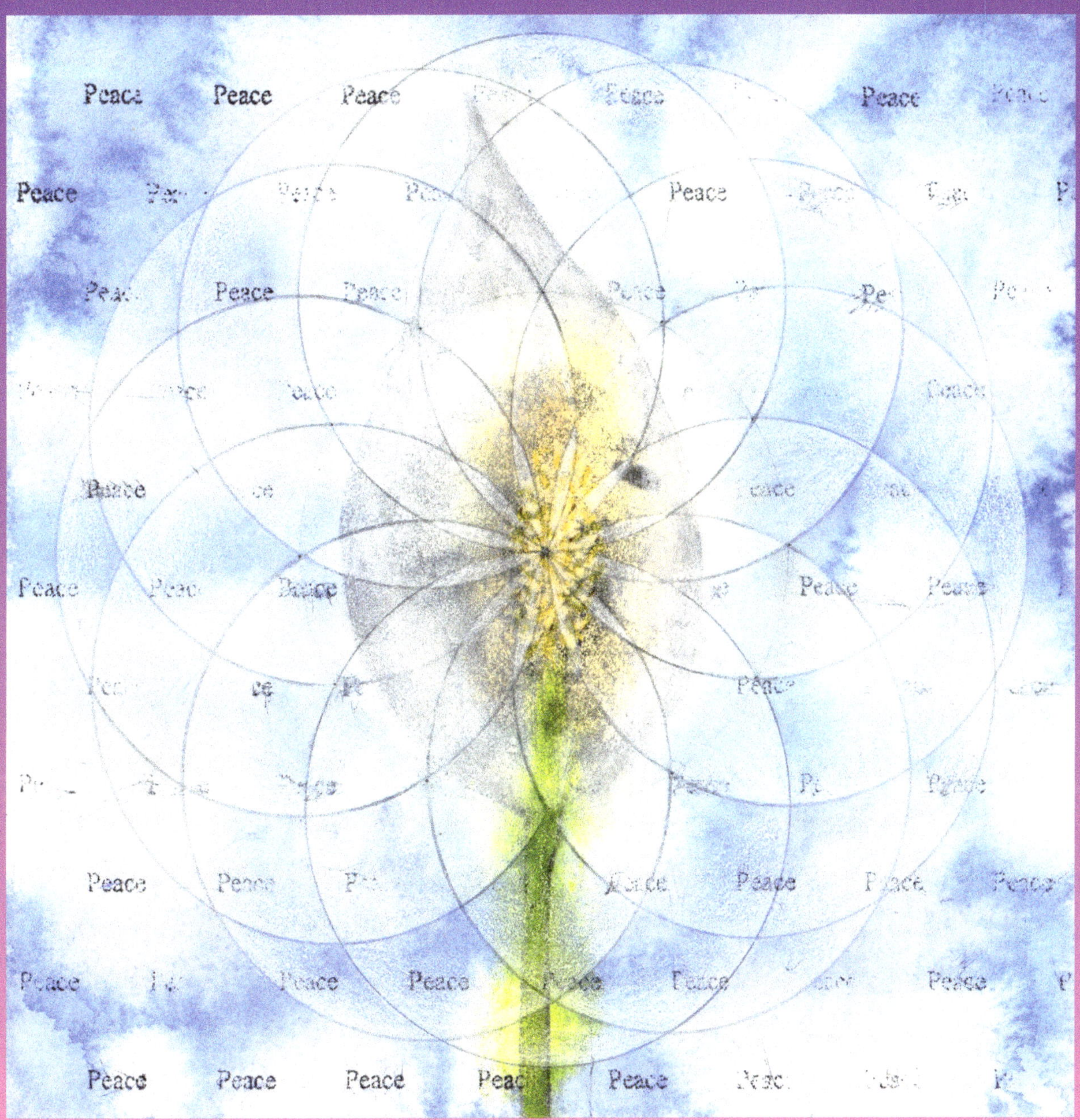

PEACE

LOVE IN THE SEED OF LIFE

In many of my mandalas
I like to represent Nature as healer.
In this mandala,
I was feeling the love for trees
and the beauty of Nature so strongly,
as well as the depth of my connection with it ALL.
How powerfully it touched and moved me
as I poured my heart into this mandala,
with enormous gratitude and appreciation.
The sacred geometry design, the Seed of Life,
has been found mysteriously
throughout the ancient world.
It is believed to symbolize the interconnection
of Nature and All on Earth.
Here it represents the beginning,
of infinite growth and becoming,
of expanding deep love,
for Nature and the Divine.

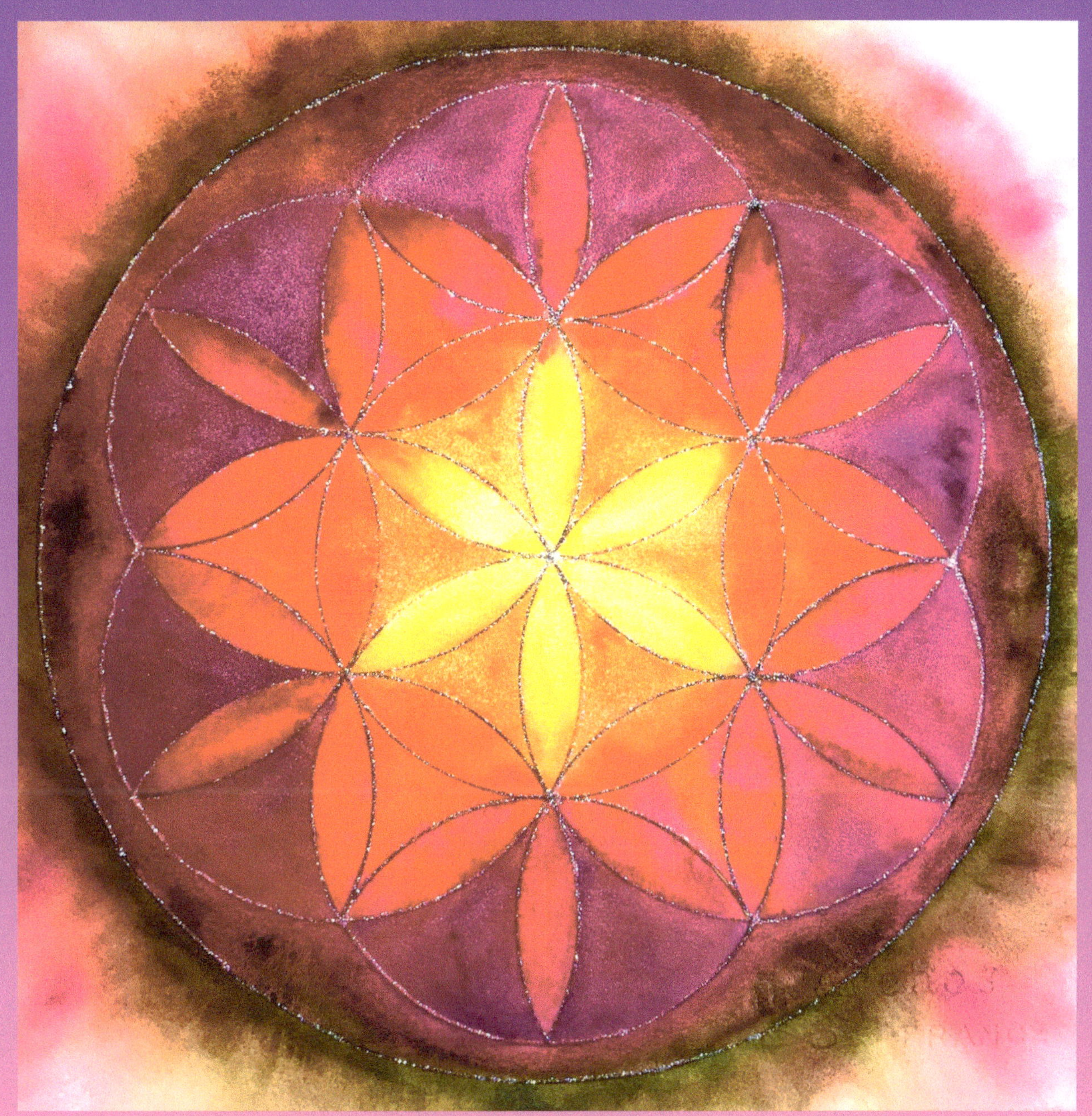

LOVE IN THE SEED OF LIFE

CONVOVULUS IS LOVE

This is a dwarf morning glory
overlaid with an ancient sacred geometry pattern.
The pattern is expanding into a
Flower of Life, but it was my first attempt,
and I hadn't quite nailed it.
The image had been floating around in my head,
but I had to be ready.
This symbol starts at the center with the Genesis pattern,
which is magically infinite and never stops.
One day at Trader Joe's I commented
on a unique necklace a cashier was wearing.
He quickly raised up his t-shirt, turned around,
and showed me the Flower of Life tattooed on his back.
A bit surprised, I told him he had just inspired me,
and I went home and began to paint this mandala.
I had been asking for messages from Spirit,
and was very excited about this connection.
I was shown that the energy of the *convovulus* flower,
the beautiful morning glory,
is very powerful and brings love,
which is never-ending.

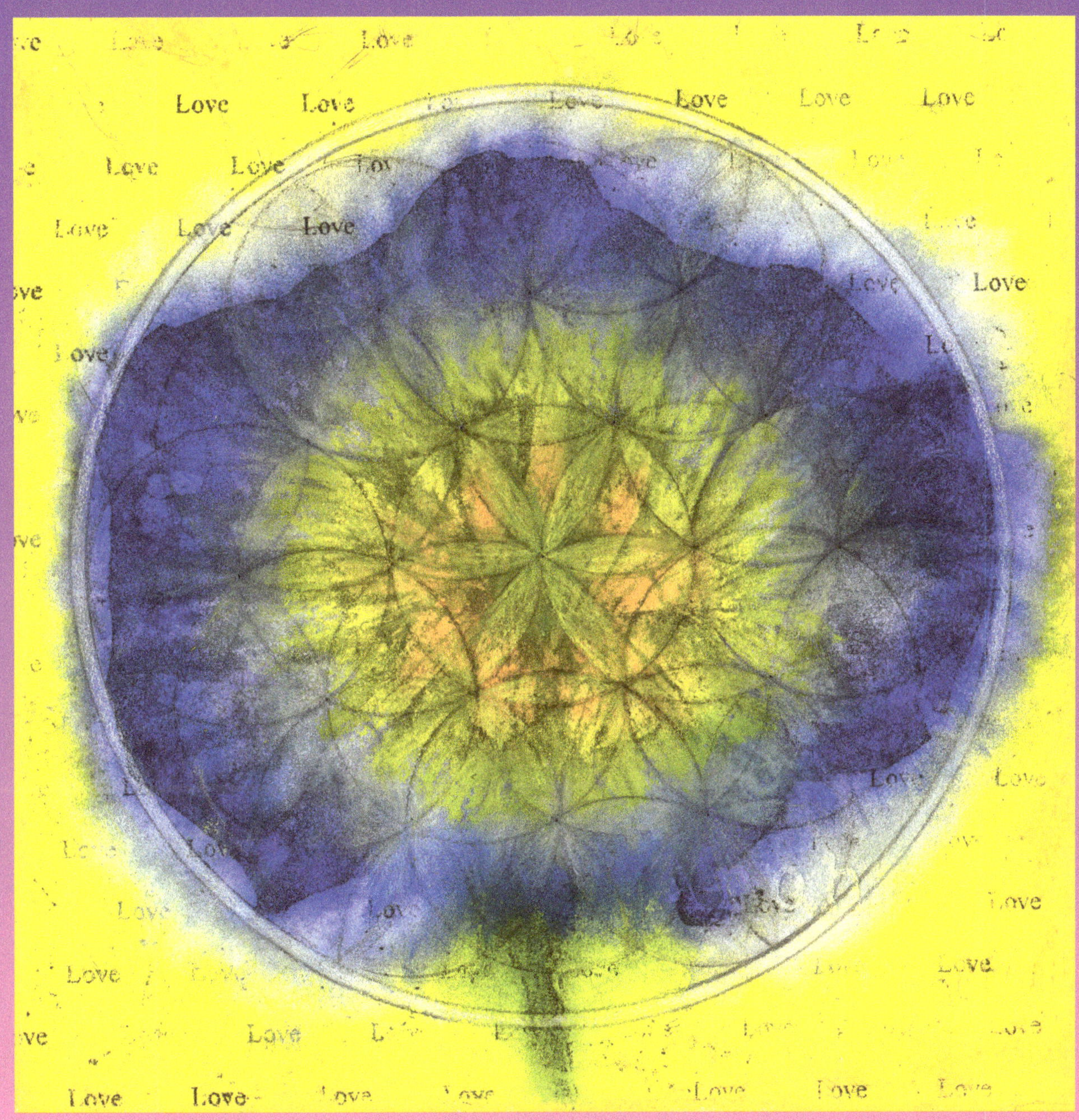

CONVOVULUS IS LOVE

YOU ARE LOVED FOR YOUR SPIRIT

A field of brightly colored cosmos flowers,
and their leaves,
told me in a vision,
You are loved for your spirit,
not for what you <u>do</u>.
The cosmos flower,
from the Greek word *kosmos,*
symbolizes the world in perfect harmony.
Presented here fluid and free,
yet centered and symmetrical,
the cosmos brought such an important message
to me and all.
It is beautiful just to be, and not have to do,
to be cared for and loved.
That is peace and wholeness,
that is perfect harmony.

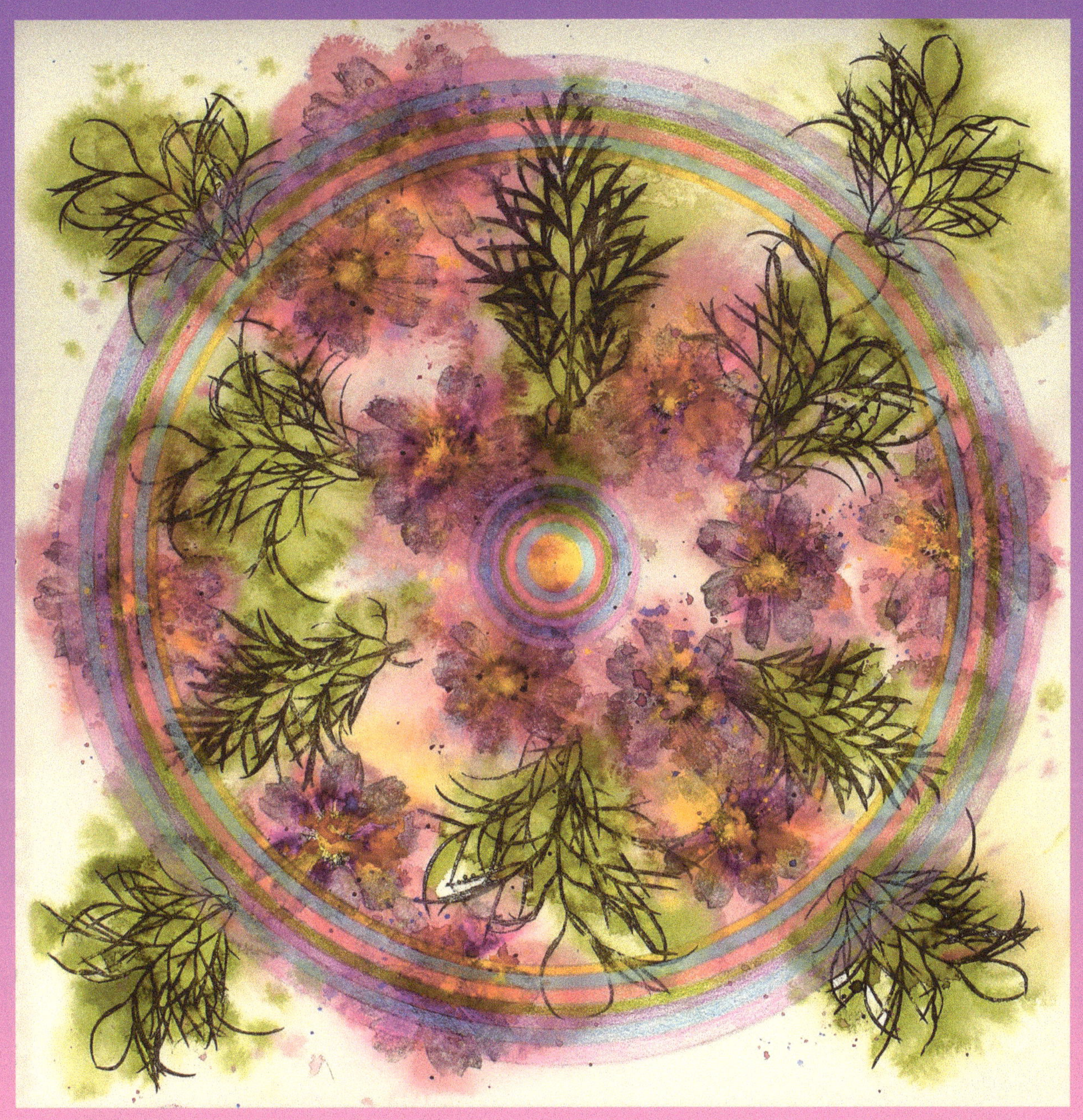

YOU ARE LOVED FOR YOUR SPIRIT

BUTTERFLIES COMFORT ME ON MY SACRED JOURNEY

Pure white flowers exploded from the butterflies,
like fireworks,
when I began to paint.
I had encountered an uncomfortable incident,
which was festering,
and I turned to my paint and paper
to create a healing mandala.
Instantaneously I saw an image of
iridescent blue butterflies surrounding red hearts.
Show me hearts and
I am transfixed!
And I needed that.
Opening to love comforted me.
That's when the beautiful white flowers
burst from the electric butterflies.
What a joy and a blessing.
I felt lighter and so much better.
Watercolor also comforts me on my journey.
For me it's Sacred.

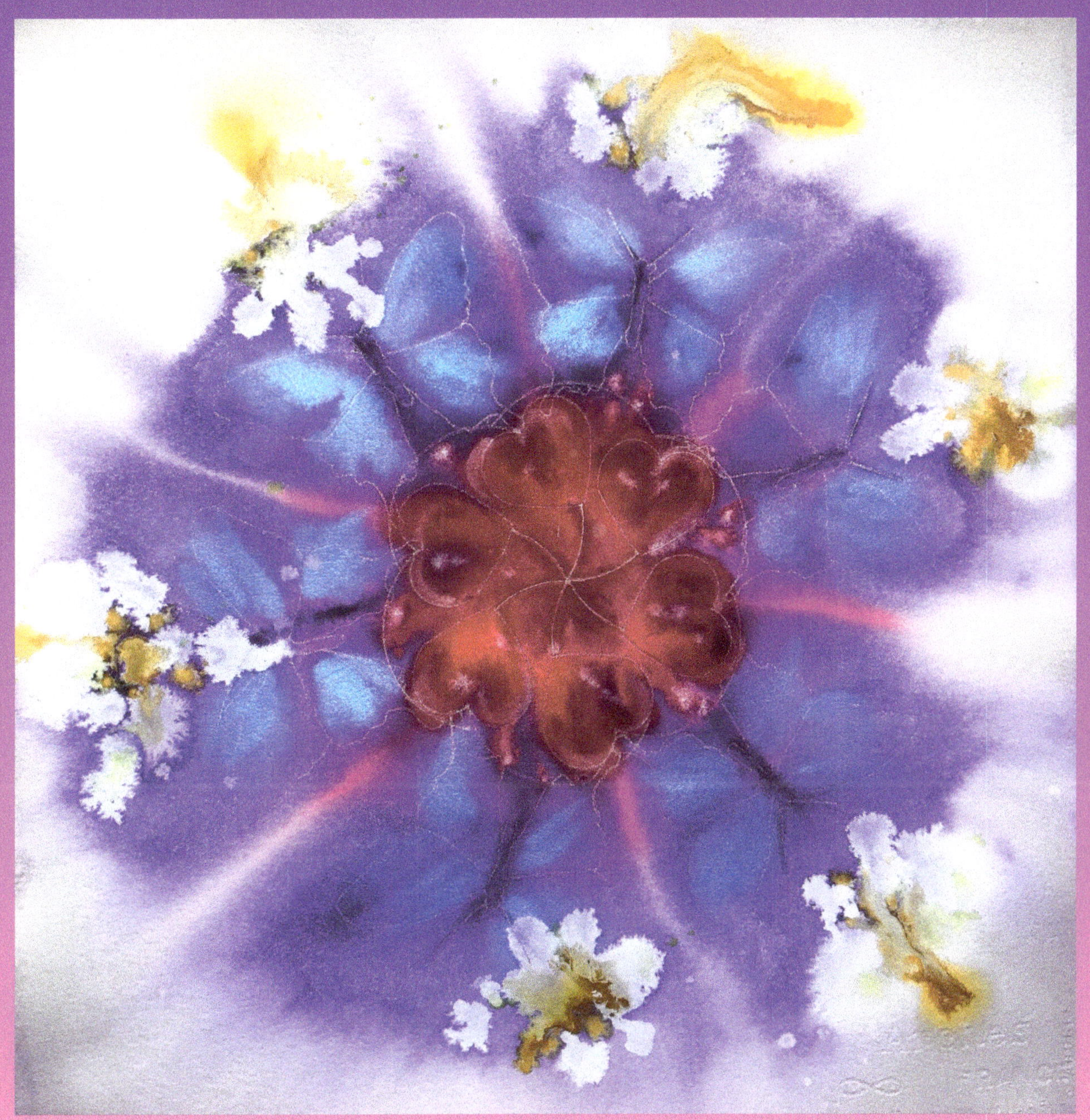

BUTTERFLIES COMFORT ME ON MY SACRED JOURNEY

HAPPY BIRTH DAY! GIVE ME FIVE!

Venus, Goddess of love and beauty,
in this mandala is a collage,
with some new additions to her stature.
For me it was reminiscent of playing with my paper dolls.
Our Venus raises her new arms in celebration
of the birth of a newly realized aspect of herself,
of becoming whole and complete.
She is celebrating the success of that.
She emerges from a confection of roses
wearing the helmet from her sister Athena,
the Goddess of wisdom and warfare.
She pats her thigh
with a "give me five."
Birds were singing loudly that day,
celebrating and feeding her with their songs.
So, it was a happy bird day, too!

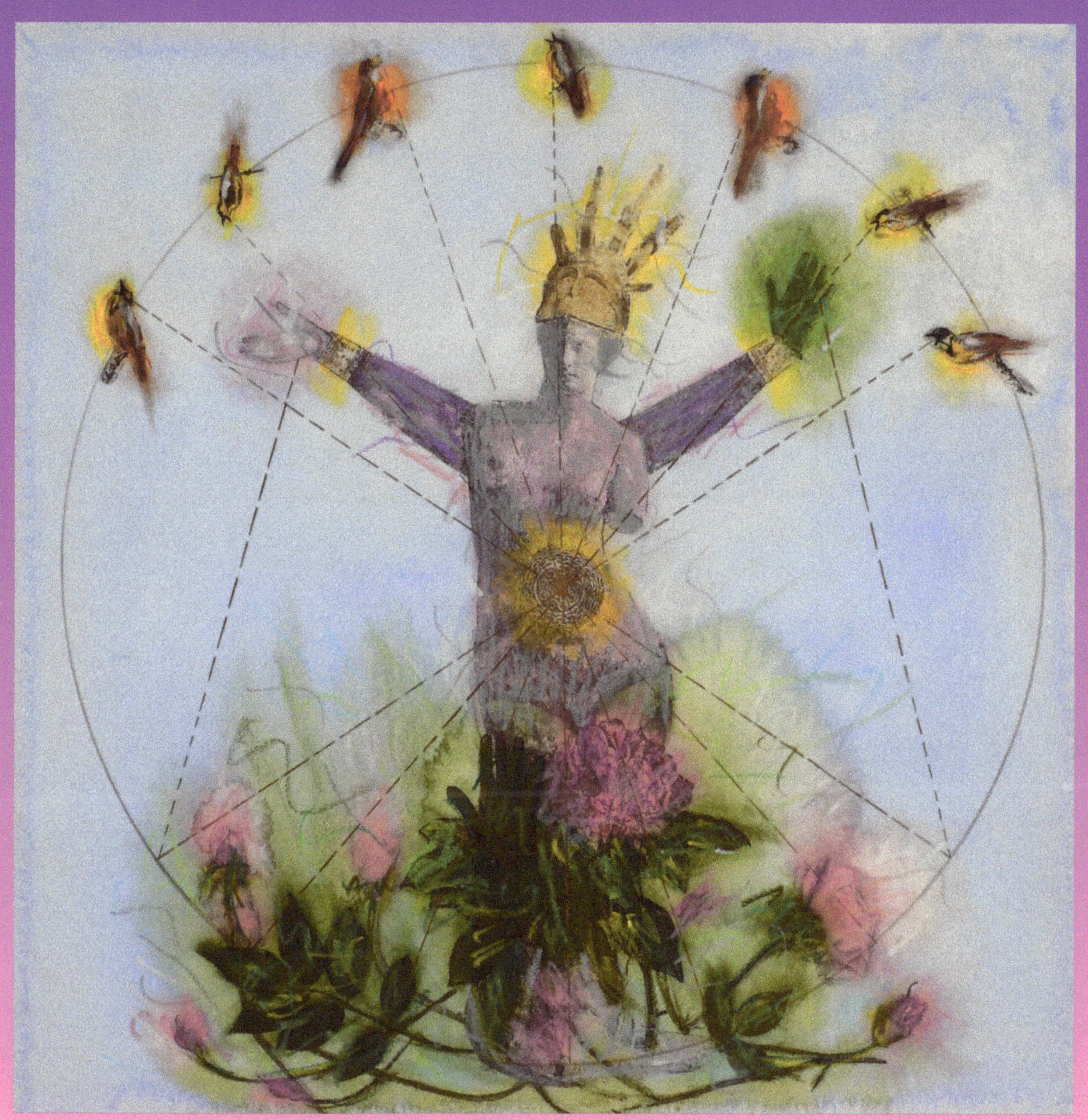

HAPPY BIRTH DAY! GIVE ME FIVE!

I AM FREE, YOU ARE FREE

Dolphins swim and jump around a Sacred Heart.
They are splashing and having fun,
like they do, it's in their nature.
The water cleanses and purifies everything.
The yellow alstroemeria, purple sage
and white calla lilies are from my garden.
These are the flowers, colors and animals I love.
Touching me deeply, they know I love them.
We all have a beautiful dance we do together.
I believe that such connections
can change our lives.
Whenever the dolphins call me to the beach,
and I see them swimming and playing,
my heart bursts with gratitude
to witness such joy and freedom.
Especially when they know I am there,
and include me in their dance.
My heart opens a little wider.
Could there be anything better?

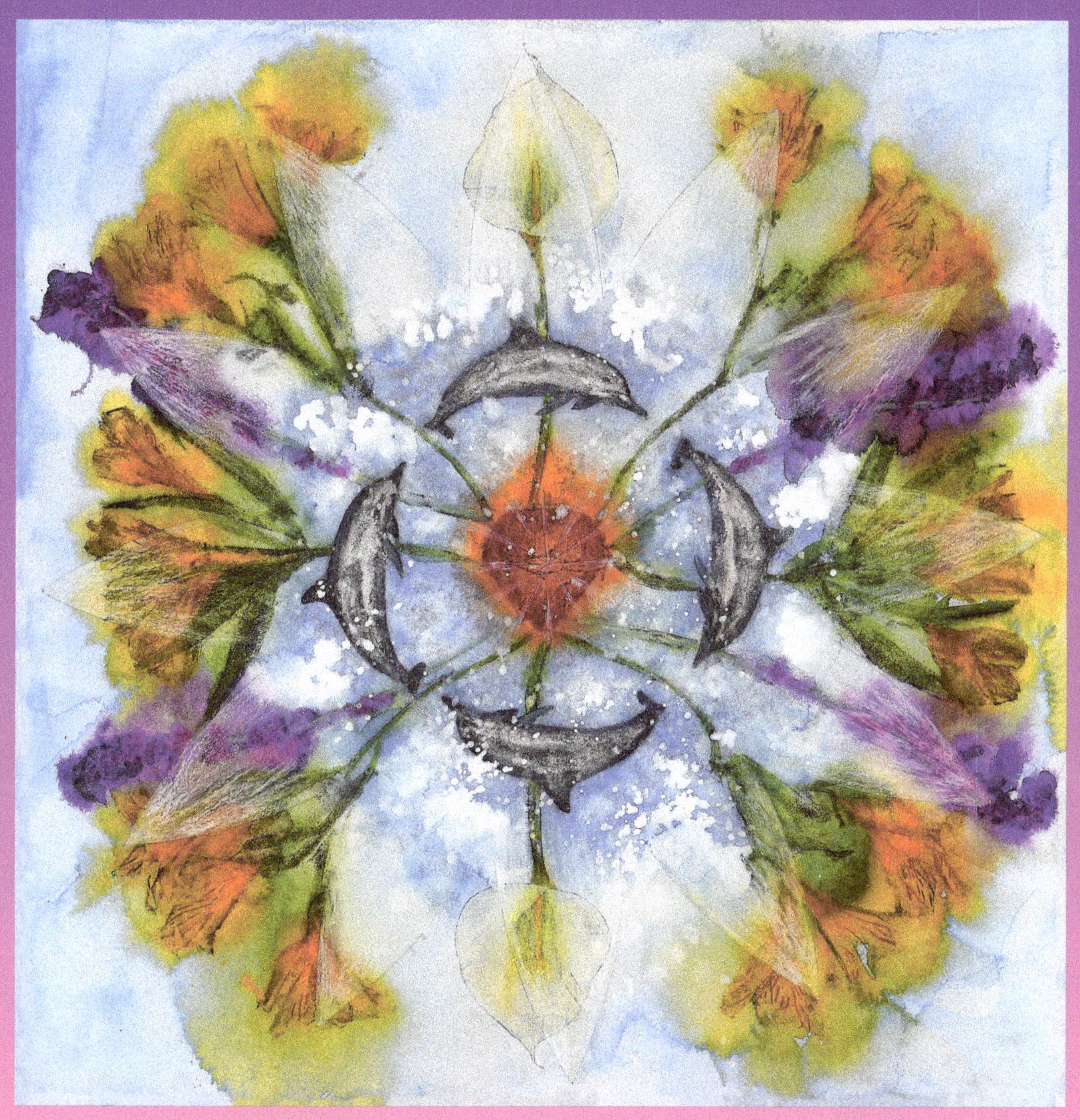

I AM FREE, YOU ARE FREE

SHE MAKES MY HEART SING

This mandala is about the love for a blue jay
who captured our hearts
and trained us to hand-feed her peanuts.
We named her Zelda,
and I painted her a special mandala,
an offering of gratitude and light for her presence.
I covered it with peanuts
as an experiment to see if
she'd go for them,
while the mandala lay on my lap.
No problem!
I am so grateful for this special relationship,
and any opportunity to connect
deeply with the wild and free in nature.
I find the beautiful energy in flowers and animals,
soothing, calming and healing,
and it connects me to the All.
And, as I began this painting, as if by magic,
an old song went through my head:
Wild Thing! You Make My Heart Sing!
When I am face to face, and eye to eye with Zelda,
she definitely makes my heart sing!

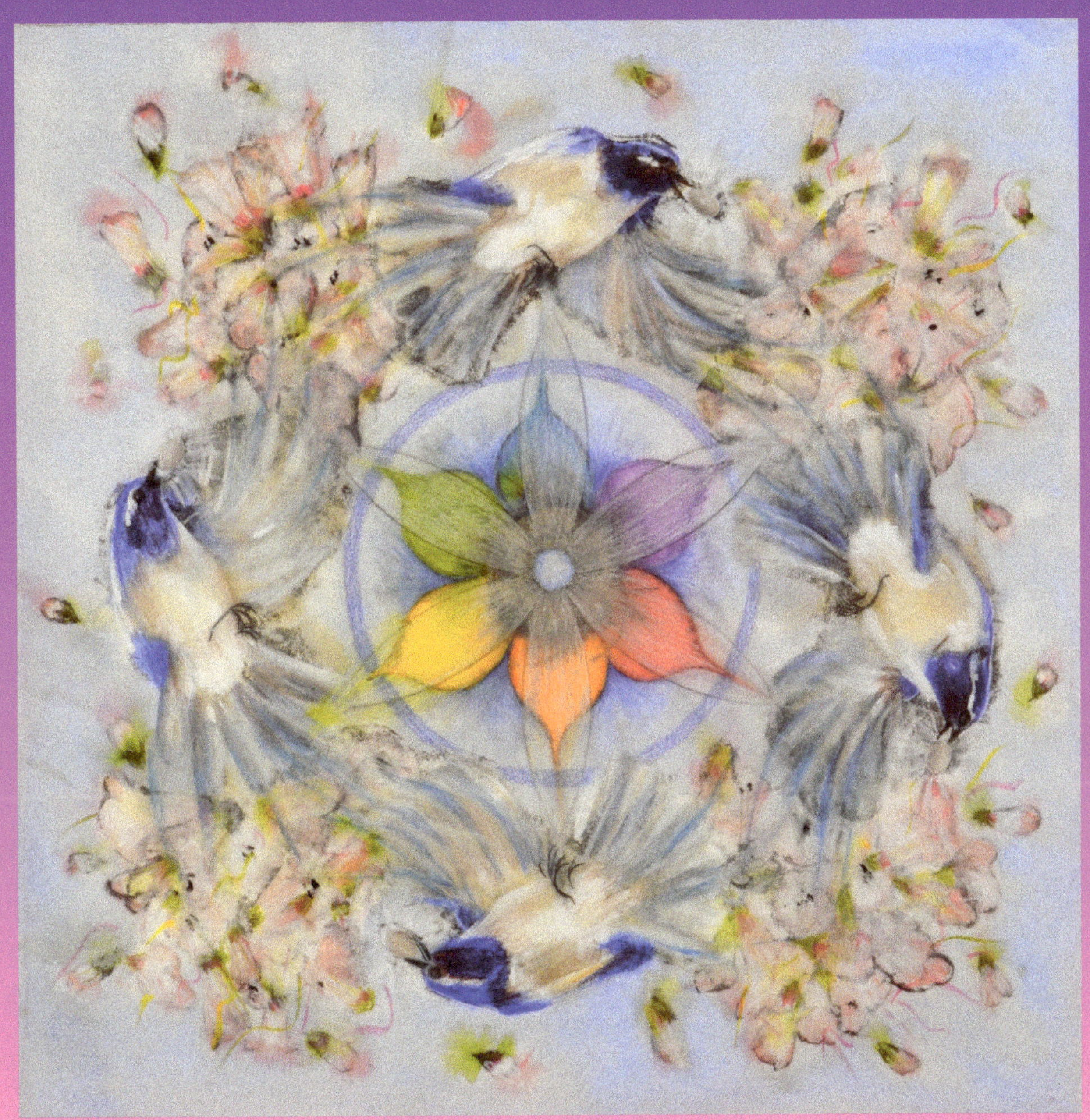

SHE MAKES MY HEART SING

SO MUCH LOVE

The vision took my breath away.
I saw so many red hearts
overflowing from my heart.
I felt such love and connection to the All
and I wanted to capture that feeling.
Before I began the mandala,
I asked Spirit for help and to co-create with me.
I always do.
I used heart shaped leaves for the hearts,
which I had gathered and dried
from a red bud tree.
The hummingbirds came
to share my joy and partake of the sweetness,
and formed a protection
around the center nest of eggs,
eggs representing new life.
The morning glory flowers swayed
and danced around the outer circle.
The final creation was adding light
radiating from the center.
I believe the mandala's message was universal—
there is so much light,
healing, joy and love
flowing,
and available for all.

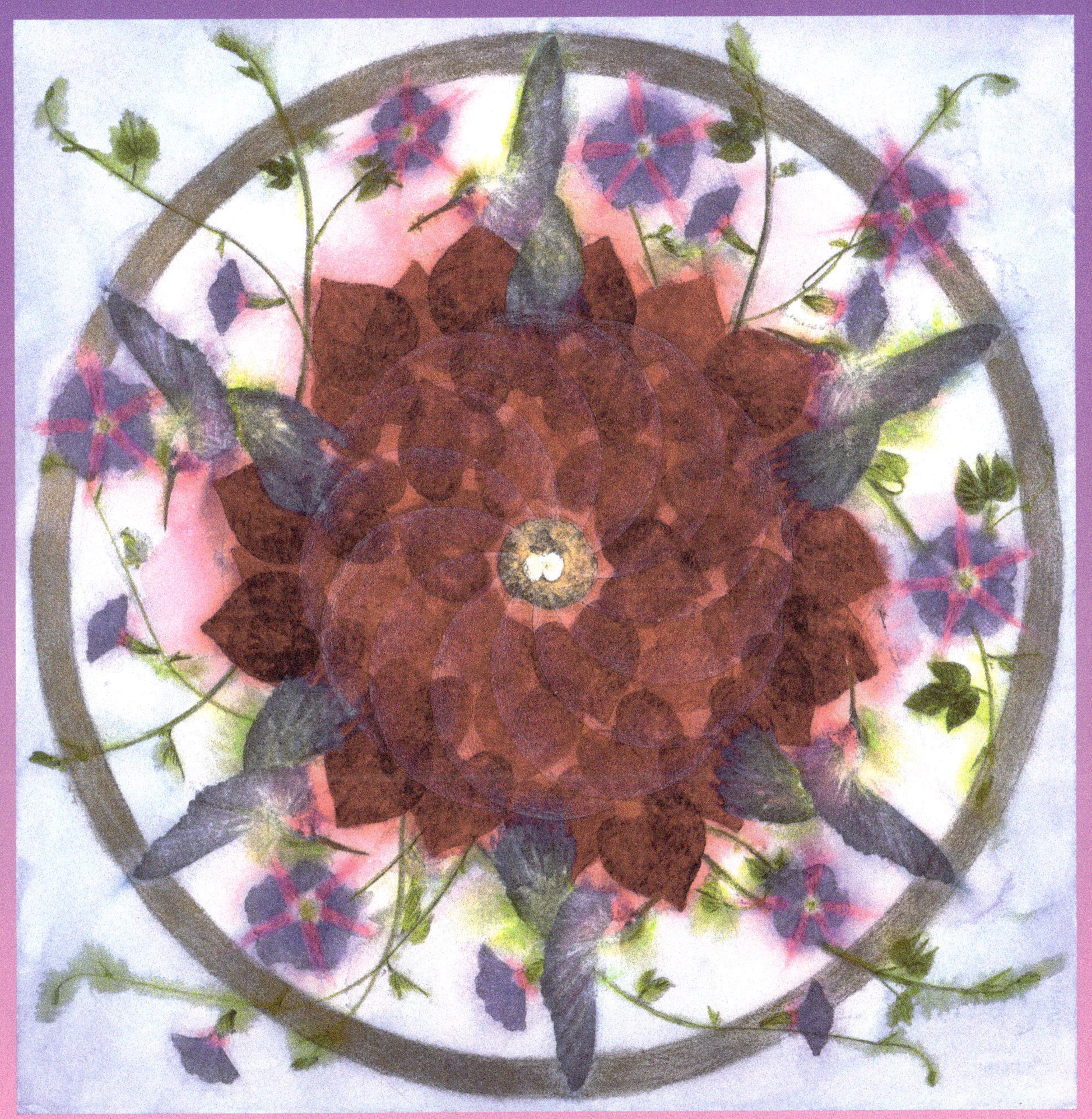

SO MUCH LOVE

Page 9   GOODNESS

Over the top of the image of a painted sunflower, are pieces of an old gouache painting of mine which I tore up and glued on. Joining the colorful scraps are mourning dove feathers at the cardinal points and dried status flowers in a circle surrounding it all. This 15" x 15" mandala is a healing mandala. Actually all mandalas, whether viewed as an observer or self-created, are healing in some way. In the luscious red and lavender center is a design drawn with a gold felt pen to assist in creating healing energies. Date: 2003.

Page 11   COMING OUT

The iris leaves and freesia flowers are coming out of a central energy, and they are protected by a grid of light. This was an image of healing for myself to be always completely safe as I opened up and came forward to be myself. It is painted with watercolor, the grid was drawn with a compass and gold pen, and the concentric circles were drawn with colored pencil. It measures 15" x 15." Date: 2003.

Page 13   BUDDING POTENTIAL

In the center of this 15" x 15" mandala is a watercolor painting of a budding agapanthus, sometimes referred to as a Lily of the Nile. It was painted loosely and freely, to simulate movement. Around the perimeter of the swirling buds are concentric rings of colored pencil and a geometric pattern drawn with a compass. My intention was to play, relax and have fun with this painting, and I definitely did! Date: 2003.

Page 15   BEING OK AND NOT WRONG

The magenta dianthus flower offered its help to me. The watercolor painting is over the top of the flowers, transferred on to hot press watercolor paper from actual photocopies of the blossoms and the sprouted leaves. The concentric circles were drawn with colored pencil. This mandala measures 15" x 15." Date: 2003.

Page 17   INTERNAL HELP

Surrounding the Divine Sacred Heart and the radiating Light in the center of this mandala, are images of beautiful, red poinsettia flowers. This 15″ x 15″ painting was painted on hot press watercolor paper with the wet on wet technique, starting with wet paper. Over the top of this sacred piece, are marks made with watercolor crayon, symbolizing the spread of Divine Energy. Date: 2003.

Page 19   GOD AS HYDRANGEA

My vision was very clear. It was a big, deep pink hydrangea blossom. I transferred an old print on to 140 lb hot press watercolor paper and painted it with the wet on wet technique, the paper fully wet. I like how the colors bleed together this way, creating soft edges. It is a tricky technique and takes practice and patience, but for me it is fun and thrilling. This 15″ x 15″ mandala was completed with colored pencil. Date: 2003.

Page 21   TWIG VISION

I made circles out of the twigs, connecting the ends together with cellophane tape. With those circles I created a loose geometric design by photocopying them and transferring copies onto hot press watercolor paper. I painted over the top of the design with watercolor, and over that painting, when it was dry, I drew the geometric design with a compass and silver felt pen. Date: 2003.

Page 23   MY SACRED SELF CHILD WITHIN

This was a class assignment I gave my mandala class and, as usual, I painted the mandala as well. It started with an image of shades of red and stars around a circle. This was from a shadow of a memory of an event when I was 3 or 4 at Christmas. I have not been able to access the event, although in time it has begun to feel like a loss or death. I painted this on a 12″ x 12″ piece of cold press watercolor paper, drew the circles and stars with a glitter gel pen, soaked the drawing in the bathtub and used the wet on wet technique with lots of pigment. The red-violet around the image came in a dream. When the piece was dry I outlined the lines with Stickles glitter glue. Date: 2019.

Page 25   FLIGHT OF THE SOUL

This mandala, with the circle of swallows, represents potential, being protected, nourished and then able to take flight. It is woven with Chinese lantern and fuchsia blossoms which were ink transfers of flowers from my garden which I transferred onto hot press watercolor paper. I built the nest from photocopies of branches and sticks. This 15" x 15" mandala was painted with my preferred technique of wet on wet onto wet paper. Date: 2004.

Page 27   NOURISHING BERRIES AND NURTURING ANEMONES

The berries were from a very old seed catalog I had and the flowers were from my garden. These colors are some of my favorites and I used a lot of watercolor pigment on the painting to get the colors very intense, using the wet on wet technique on wet hot press paper. There are touches of colored pencil, first in the center and then enhancing the other images. This mandala is 15" x 15." Date: 2005.

Page 29   CAMELLIA IS CARING

I learned from an energy dowser that a photograph of a flower carries the same energy as the live flower. I had sensed that myself, and therefore used photos or photocopies of flowers during a phase of my painting mandalas. This is an actual camellia from my garden, photocopied and incorporated into the mandala, with a golden star over the top of it and a concentric circle of colored pencil. The word "caring" repeats in this mandala which measures 6" x 6." I started a series of small mandalas which included words during the time I was writing my first book and did not have the time to paint big mandalas. They were fun to do and I just couldn't *not* paint! Date: 2007.

Page 31   DYING TO BE BORN ANEW

This piece is a 15" x 15" watercolor painted over ink transfers with a touch of gold paint at the center, and the sacred geometry symbol, called the Seed of Life, in pink colored pencil. My husband loves this mandala and calls it "an artful transition of death and rebirth." It is another wet on wet painting done on wet hot press watercolor paper. Date: 2005.

Page 33   SNOWBALL, INSPIRE THE BLUEBIRD TO SING MY SWEETNESS INTO BEING

A bluebird is perched on a branch of a snowball bush, within the sacred geometry symbol called the *vesica piscis*, literally "bladder of the fish." The shape is also called a *mandorla*, or almond. It is centered in the middle of several concentric circles. When I spotted the bluebird, it WAS the first time I had ever seen one in our area. The mandala is created with ink transfers and energies, watercolor, colored pencil and oil pastel and measures 15" x 15." Date: 2006.

Page 35   BURNING AWAY DEFEAT

A sacred geometry pattern, often called a Torus, centers itself over the top of a fully blooming parrot tulip. Tomato slices are floating above the tulip and all are in flames.Watercolor was applied over ink transfers with the wet on wet technique onto wet hot press watercolor paper, then colored pencil and finally oil pastel were applied. This is a small mixed media painting, just 7.5" x 7.5." Date: 2009.

Page 37   GO FOR IT

Over the upright white calla lilies is a geometric flower in pink pencil. The word "Life" is repeated in the background. Watercolor and gouache are painted over the ink transfers with a wet on wet technique on wet hot press watercolor paper. Colored pencil and oil pastel were added to finalize the work. The original is a small piece, about 7" x 7." Date: 2009.

Page 39   STEP OUT OF THE DARKNESS AND INTO THE LIMELIGHT

Rings of light are drawn with white pencil over the circle of leaves. Wet on wet watercolor is painted over ink transfers onto hot press watercolor paper and then accented with colored pencil. Also a small one, this mandala is 8.5" x 8.5." Date: 2010.

Page 41   FIRST CHAKRA CIRCLE OF LOVE

I painted a 7" Circle of Love for each of seven chakras, energy centers in our energy body. This was for a Mandalas and Alchemy class I taught. I like to do the assignments right along with the participants. I drew the image of the first chakra, which is red in color, with a glitter gel pen and painted over the drawing with the wet on wet technique, and the cold press watercolor paper was entirely wet. I started the drawing on an 8" square piece of paper, drew the circle on it with a compass, painted it and cut it out with scissors when it was dry. Date: 2019.

Page 43   NURTURING TURTLE

Mother Turtle was created by collaging pieces of all species of turtles together to make a whole, one of a kind. I painted over the transferred collage with the wet on wet technique with the entire hot press watercolor paper wet. Over the top of the dry painting, starting at the center, I drew what is called the Genesis pattern (what generates it) of the Seed of Life, a very ancient sacred geometry pattern which will infinitely repeat. This painting is 15" x 15." Date: 2005.

Page 45   GRATITUDE

Dried heart leaves from a red bud tree, heavenly bamboo leaves and Japanese maple leaves were all laid upon the watercolor painting of transferred images of flowers and leaves. My favorite, the wet on wet technique with the entire paper wet, was used on hot press watercolor paper. The Flower of Life at the center was drawn with a fine gold pen. The pen leaked a bit leaving some gold blobs. I left them as is. Nothing is perfect! I added some dots of Stickles glitter glue to the symbol. Colored pencil was added to the imagery before the leaves were placed and glued down. The mandala measures 15" x 15." Date: 2015.

Page 47   BLOOM! YOU ARE FREE

That's exactly what I had written on the back of this mandala, "The star cried out, 'Bloom! You are free.'" The star and the surrounding green leaves and pink flowers are from images of upholstery fabric I transferred onto hot press watercolor paper. I painted over the top of that, using the wet on wet technique on wet paper. When it was dry I added colored pencil and oil pastel. This piece measures 15" x 15." Date: 2007.

Page 49 TRANSFORMATION: IN THE LAND OF THE FREE & HOME OF THE BRAVE

What was I thinking when I created this mandala? I usually will write on the back of the paper my intention for the piece. Typically I write: I intend to co-create with spirit a mandala of love and healing...and follow with details of what I intend to paint. I like to put my hand in the hand of Spirit and create with the help of a higher vision. When I finish the painting I also like to write notes on the back about the experience. However, this painting did not have an intention, nor any notes—just the title and date, which I usually write religiously on any work. That is all I know. This large, 22" x 22," mandala on hot press paper was painted with watercolor and gouache over ink transfers with the wet on wet technique and the paper entirely wet. It was completed with colored pencil and oil pastel. Date: 2006.

Page 51   HEALING WITH ROSES; LOOKING TO SEE WHO I REALLY AM

So much energy comes from the roses and leaves of my rose trees. This 15″ x 15″ mandala was painted over the top of the ink transfers of the bunny and roses, with the wet on wet technique onto hot press watercolor paper. The white geometric flower and the ring of color at the center were drawn with a compass and filled in with colored pencil. Colored pencil highlights the roses and leaves. Date: 2003.

Page 53   THE HEALING FROM THE BROMELIAD

I painted this mandala with free flowing and spontaneous strokes on top of the wet on wet watercolor sky blue background. It was fun and loose for me, a letting go. Over the top of the dry painting I drew a geometric design with a compass and a white colored pencil. It measures 15″ x 15.″ Date: 2004.

Page 55   CYCLAMENS COMING OUT OF A BIG HEART

Do you see the "vase," in the shape of a big heart rock? I transferred a copy of an enlarged heart rock on to wet hot press watercolor paper, painting the mandala in my favorite technique of wet on wet. I had lightly drawn the cyclamen leaves and blossoms on the paper and when I painted them, on the wet paper, they bled just as I wanted them to. It was fun! Over the top of the dry painting, I drew a geometric pattern with a compass and a white pencil. This mandala measures 15″ x 15.″ Date: 2004.

Page 57   BUDDING

Lots of different colored iris buds are standing upright and together, with the word "Budding" around them. They are painted with the wet on wet technique on wet hot press watercolor paper. Geometric flowers float over the top of the iris buds, each in a different color created by colored pencil, and I loved coloring them rather than using white as I'd always done before. This small mandala measures 71/2″ x 71/2.″ Date: 2009.

Page 59   PASSION

One freesia blossom is surrounded by lots of freesia buds. It glows from a circle of geometry at its center. The colors are like fire and flames. Over the top of transferred images I painted with the wet on wet technique on wet hot press watercolor paper. The word "Passion" floats among the images. Colored pencil and oil pastel were added to finish this 7 1/2″ x 7 1/2″ mandala. Date: 2008.

I saw a performance of works of art created to heal trauma, and it moved me very deeply. This mandala was inspired by those artists and came from a vision I had of helleborus flowers overlaid with a gold drawing of the Flower of Life. Over ink transfers I used the wet on wet watercolor technique on wet hot press paper. Next came colored pencil and the Flower of Life drawn with a gold felt pen and a compass. I read that some dried helleborus flowers are poison and used as a heart stimulant, which I found interesting and relevant. The mandala measures 15" x 15." Date: 2016.

Page 63   FEEL IT TO HEAL IT

Painted over transferred flowers and the words "Feel" and "Feelings," I used my favorite technique, wet on wet, on wet hot press watercolor paper. I drew the geometric pattern with a compass and a white colored pencil after it was dry. This small mandala measures 7" x 7." Date: 2008.

Page 65   SHOW HER WHAT HELPS

Using the playful and fun wet on wet watercolor technique, I painted over the top of transferred images of flowers and the words "Help" onto wet hot press paper. Onto the dry images I used colored pencil on the 7.5" x 7.5" mandala. I like this painting and message so much that I have used it on some of my business cards. Date: 2009.

Page 67   THERE IS A HEALING GOING ON

The Genesis pattern of the Flower of Life is at the center of this 7" x 7" mandala, it is called that because it generates a symbol which can repeat infinitely. I used my favored wet on wet watercolor technique on wet hot press paper over the symbol and the "Healing" words. On the dry painting I used colored pencil and oil pastel smudged with an eraser. Date: 2007.

Page 69   THOUGHTS ARE THINGS

Over the words "Thoughts," the ink transfers and the geometric drawing, I painted with my fun favorite, the wet on wet watercolor technique, onto wet hot press watercolor paper. On top of the dry 7.5" x 7.5" mandala, I applied colored pencil. Date: 2009.

Page 71   NURTURE ME WHERE I LIVE AND LET ME FLY

Over the top of transferred images, I used the wet on wet watercolor technique on wet hot press paper. I incorporated some gouache watercolor as well. When this 15" x 15" mandala was dry I applied colored pencil and oil pastel. The circle around the image is gold colored pencil. I just noticed that the first time I tried an ink transfer was on a pelvic bone and I used turpentine with my hands which is not such a good idea. (Now I use a Chartpak Blender.) I had been inspired years earlier by a show I saw of Robert Rauschenberg's work, a very well known modern American artist. I loved the quality of the images with his big transfers and I knew one day I would try it myself, even though I didn't know how he did it. The mandala with the first transferred pelvic bone is called "Please Receive My Suffering" and is in my first book *Art in My Heart: The Power of Watercolor Mandala Making*. Date: 2006.

Page 73   RELEASE

In the center of this mandala is a sacred geometry symbol called the Genesis pattern. The Genesis pattern is what creates the Seed of Life, which, when expanded, creates the Egg of Life and when that is expanded it becomes the Flower of Life. I imagined that the circle was spinning, which created the releasing energy. I painted this 7.5" x 7.5" mandala with my playful wet on wet technique over wet hot press watercolor paper over transferred images and the words "Release." This was such a fun image and very fun to paint. I added colored pencil after the painting was dry. Date: 2008.

Page 75   THE FLOWERING OF ENCOURAGEMENT

This little gem measures 8.5" x 8.5" and the transferred flowers are overpainted with the wet on wet watercolor technique I prefer. A mixture of watercolor and gouache were applied to wet hot press paper. I drew the geometric flower at the center with a white colored pencil and a compass on the dry mandala. Oil pastel was added last. Date: 2009.

Page 77   AMARYLLIS, ANEMONE, LETTUCE AND THE NEED FOR STARS

I painted over the top of transferred images with the wet on wet watercolor technique on wet hot press paper. The square design within the circle comes from Eastern mandalas and is representative of a temple with four portals and the four directions. The square design was drawn with colored pencil as were the concentric circles. This mandala measures 15" x 15." Date: 2005.

Page 79   REACHING FOR THE LIGHT

I'm crazy about yellow calla lilies! Using my favored technique of wet on wet on wet hot press watercolor paper, I painted over the transferred images and the words "Reach." The geometric circle pattern was added, after the painting dried, with a compass and blue colored pencil. This mandala measures 7.5" x 7.5." Date: 2008.

Page 81   THE OFFERING: OLIVE BRANCHES, LIMELIGHT AND THE STAR

This little gem measures 7.5" x 7.5" and was painted with the technique I most always use, wet on wet onto wet hot press watercolor paper. I painted over the transferred foliage and the words "Offering." Over the dry painting I drew the geometric circles with a compass and blue colored pencil. Date: 2009.

Page 83   EXPANDING MY KALEIDOSCOPE VISION

This bold undertaking measures 15" x 15," was drawn with a compass, ruler and a glitter pen. The drawing was soaked for 15 minutes, in the bathtub, before I started adding paint, wet on wet style, onto the cold press 140 lb Arches watercolor paper. To keep the colors bold, I continued to add a bit of watercolor pigment fresh from the tubes. After it was dry, I retraced the lines with the glitter pen. Why the stars? They just wanted to be there, it was a celebration. I call paintings done like this "Bathtub Beauties." I find the process very exciting! Date: 2018.

Page 85   BEAUTIFUL, SWEET AND MYSTERIOUS

This sweet 7.5" x 7.5" mandala was painted with my favored and fun wet on wet technique on wet hot press watercolor paper. The transferred images and "Beautiful" words were overpainted, and when the painting was dry, I drew the geometric flower, with a compass and a pink colored pencil, over the top of the big orchid. Date: 2008.

Page 87   MY EGG OF LIFE

This mandala was painted on a 12" x 12" piece of 140 lb cold press paper which was soaked in the bathtub after I drew the design with a compass and glitter gel pen. I painted with watercolor and mica watercolor with the wet on wet technique I so love—using lots of pigment! After the mandala was dry, I went over the 6 petals in each circle with a fine gold felt pen and added more mica paint to each petal. Date: 2020.

Page 89   FREE

This special small mandala measures 7" x 7," and is painted with watercolor and gouache over transferred images and the words "Free" onto wet hot press paper. The geometric radiating flower was drawn with a compass and lead pencil. Colored pencil and oil pastel was added last. I liked this mandala so much that I put it on the back of some my business cards. Date: 2008.

Page 91   PEACE

I love painting blue skies and clouds. They appear in many of my mandalas. This mandala, with its special message, measures 7" x 7" and was painted on hot press paper using the wet on wet technique on wet paper. Watercolor and gouache were used over the top of the transferred image and "Peace" words. Colored pencil finished the piece. Date: 2006.

Page 93   LOVE IN THE SEED OF LIFE

I drew the Seed of Life with a compass and a glitter gel pen. I then soaked the 12" x 12" piece in the bathtub and painted over the top of the drawing using lots of watercolor and mica watercolor pigment on cold press 140 lb Arches paper. After the mandala was dry, I used Stickle's glitter glue to outline the Seed of Life drawing. Very fun and satisfying! Date: 2017.

Page 95   CONVOVULUS IS LOVE

I drew the geometry symbol, using a compass and lead pencil, over the dry painting which had been done with the wet on wet technique on wet hot press paper. I painted with watercolor over the transferred images of the flower and the words "Love." This 7" x 7" mandala was finished with colored pencil. Date: 2007.

Page 97   YOU ARE LOVED FOR YOUR SPIRIT

This 15" x 15" mandala of bright and happy cosmos from my garden, was painted over transferred images on wet hot press watercolor paper with the fun, wet on wet technique. Over the top of the dry painting I created concentric circles at the center and outside ring with colored pencil. Date: 2003.

Page 99   BUTTERFLIES COMFORT ME ON MY SACRED JOURNEY

I drew the butterflies and hearts with a glitter gel pen on a 15" x 15" square of 140 lb cold press watercolor paper. I soaked the drawing in the bathtub and painted it dripping wet. Dicey! I applied lots of watercolor pigment, mica watercolor and white gouache. I love this form of the wet on wet technique, it thrills me. Date: 2019.

Page 101   HAPPY BIRTH DAY! GIVE ME FIVE!

This fun 15" x 15" mandala was overpainted with watercolor and gouache on to wet hot press paper using the wet on wet approach over the transferred images. The connecting lines between Venus' center and the birds were drawn with a gold pen. Colored pencil and oil pastel were added when the painting was dry. Date: 2006.

Page 103   I AM FREE, YOU ARE FREE

On a 15" x 15" piece of wet hot press paper, I painted over the transferred images with watercolor, gouache and mica watercolor using my favorite wet on wet technique. When it was dry I applied colored pencil and oil pastel. Completely over the top I added a flower-like geometry drawing with a compass and white pencil. Date: 2013.

Page 105   SHE MAKES MY HEART SING

Using an actual photo of Zelda, I created a collage and transferred it, along with images of an Apple Blossom penstemon and the peanut mandala, onto a 15" x 15" piece of hot press paper. I painted it wet with watercolor, gouache and metallic watercolor using the wet on wet technique. When it was dry I applied colored pencil and oil pastel. I created a fun video of photos and video clips of her on YouTube called "Mandala for a Blue Jay" on MicheleFaiaMandalas. Date: 2013.

Page 107   SO MUCH LOVE

This beauty was painted on a wet 15" x 15" piece of hot press paper over the top of the transferred images, and with the flowing wet on wet technique, using watercolor, gouache and mica watercolor. Colored pencil and oil pastel were added when the mandala was dry. The spiraling circle was done with a compass and a white pencil over the top of the red hearts. It was such a joy to create this mandala! Date: 2018.

ACKNOWLEDGEMENTS

Thank you Joanne Young for suggesting I write this book and for your support to be "brave," and thank you Peggy Black and 'the team' for helping me clear my inner obstacles and be ready for my "shift." Thank you my Divine Family for your unwavering spiritual guidance, inspiration and communication. Thank you Don Faia, my awesome, supportive artist husband, for your years of believing in and encouraging me, and your amazing design of this and all my books. Thank you Marda Reid for your jubilant and enthusiastic reactions to previewing my work, which kept me going, and thank you Bonno Bernard for your steady, unwavering expertise in formatting what you called "holy work," for publication. Thank you Mom and Dad for teaching me the extreme fulfillment of growing flowers and gardening, and thank you flowers for your love, beauty, inspiration, guidance, deep connection and ready messages – you ever-gladden my heart! Thank you watercolors for filling my heart with such joy in my chosen "work," and thank you Mandalas for giving me a spiritual ground in which to delve into the great mystery – of the Center, of Life, of Light, of the Heart.

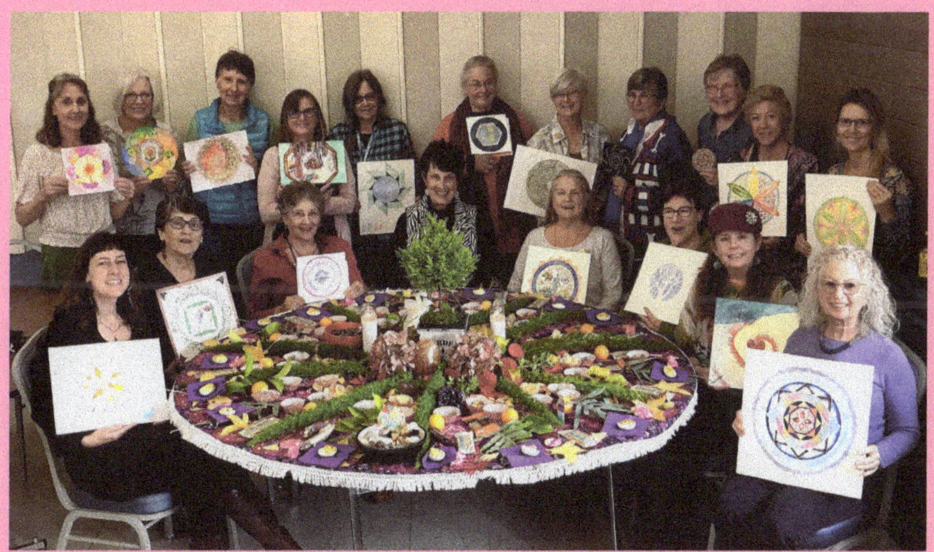

Thank you all my students and fellow Mandala Makers, you, through the years, have believed in me. You sparked my own on-going growth, depth and continued amazement of the wonderful and powerful ancient tool the Mandala. I would not be where I am without you!

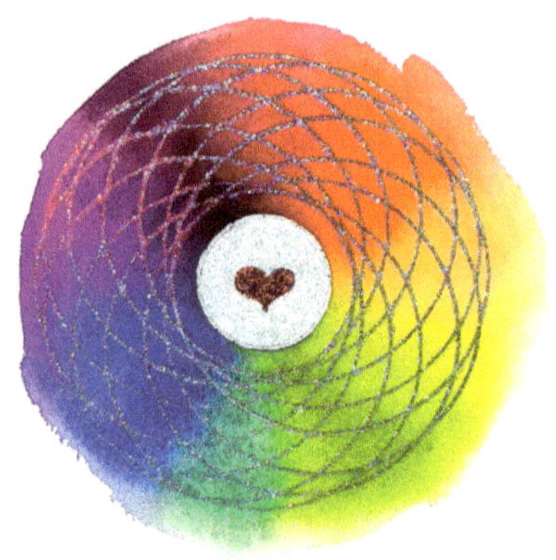

www.michelefaia.com

www.ingramcontent.com/pod-product-compliance
Lightning Source LLC
Chambersburg PA
CBHW041032050726
47599CB00018B/1936